Lynn Triplett

CRISIS POLITICS IN PREWAR JAPAN

A *Monumenta Nipponica*
Monograph

Crisis Politics in Prewar Japan

INSTITUTIONAL AND IDEOLOGICAL

PROBLEMS OF THE 1930s

Editor: GEORGE M. WILSON

Contributors:

BEN-AMI SHILLONY

RICHARD J. SMETHURST

ROBERT M. SPAULDING, JR.

GEORGE M. WILSON

PUBLISHED BY

SOPHIA UNIVERSITY, TOKYO

PUBLISHED BY

SOPHIA UNIVERSITY

7 KIOI-CHŌ, CHIYODA-KU

TOKYO, 102

PRINTED IN JAPAN

THE VOYAGERS' PRESS, TOKYO

Preface

GIVING rise to this volume was a conviction shared by the authors that Japan in the 1930s has not received the full measure of attention it deserves in Western—or Japanese—scholarship: most accounts have treated the decade more as a 'prelude to war' than as a period of development and change in its own right.

The papers presented here were originally delivered in briefer form at a panel chaired by Professor James B. Crowley of Yale University, held in Boston during the 1969 annual meeting of the Association for Asian Studies. Since that time, the authors have made extensive revisions, but we retain our original conviction that the crisis-ridden years of the 1930s demand more attention, and we hope that these studies will improve our general understanding of Japanese political processes during those years.

Many people have assisted in making this book possible. Particular thanks go to Fr. Edmund Skrzypczak and the *Monumenta Nipponica* staff in Tokyo, who edited and set the volume promptly and accurately. I should also like to thank Mr. Thomas E. Swann, Cambridge, Massachusetts, who first suggested this format for the papers and who read all of the materials before transmitting them to Tokyo. Finally, our appreciation goes to Professors Grant Goodman and Arthur Tiedemann for their encouragement and suggestions for improvement. None of the above persons is to blame for errors that may remain; for them the authors bear sole responsibility.

April 1970

GEORGE M. WILSON
Bloomington, Indiana

Contents

Introduction

SCHOLARS looking back on the decade of the 1930s in Japan have tended to evaluate events in terms of their real or apparent contribution to the Japanese 'drift' toward the Pacific War. This tendency among both Japanese and Western writers to list out a set of dates as 'milestones' or 'signposts' along the road leading to the war has sometimes deterred us from examining what was actually taking place. In other words, we have often fallen far short of understanding what the meaning of events was for those who lived through them.

This monograph incorporates three articles and an essay which seek to overcome the 'leading up to war' syndrome and to illuminate the internal workings of some of the political crises that occurred so often in Japan during the 1930s. Each author focuses on a distinct problem, but taken together the articles provide a cross section of politics at the time. The stress in this volume is on institutions: the three articles (by Messrs. Smethurst, Shillony, and Spaulding) have as their central subjects a pressure group, a rebellious military force, and a wing of the civil bureaucracy. But all of the studies in this monograph, including my essay at the end, also afford us glimpses of the play of ideas in the working out of political history during the 1930s.

Mr. Smethurst's topic is the Military Reserve Association and its role in the crisis that arose in 1935 concerning Professor Minobe Tatsukichi's[1] theory that the emperor was an 'organ' of the Japanese state. Today we can see what most Japanese leaders saw at the time: that Minobe's was a legal interpretation of the emperor's place in the Japanese system of government, and that the professor was only stating in legalistic terms what was an obvious fact of political life. The emperor did not make policy, yet he did have an important role in legitimizing it because all public policy was issued in his name. He

---

1 美濃部達吉

was, in the words of contemporary political analysis, the key to the Japanese government's symbolic capability.[2] And the public was extremely responsive to the emperor's symbolic authority. So when, in 1935, politicians and journalists turned their knives against Minobe, the public responded by joining in to discredit him and his theory as inimical to the proper interests of Japan. Minobe's view of the emperor was, in effect, labeled 'un-Japanese': it seemed to clash with the Meiji Constitution, which stipulated that the emperor was the direct source of all authority, and with the *kokutai*—the central characteristics of the Japanese political tradition, according to which the emperor was superior to other mortals and by hereditary custom was sovereign over the Japanese nation.

Pressure groups added their voices to the general clamor against the Minobe theory, and the most vociferous lobbyist attack came from the far-flung Military Reserve Association, which had branches all over the country and engaged in a wide variety of educational (that is, propaganda) activities designed to boost the army and navy and to promote military values among the general public. One of the most interesting points Mr. Smethurst makes is that local reservists, less sophisticated and less aware of the real workings of Japanese national politics, were far more rabid in denouncing the emperor-organ theory than were the leaders of the association's central headquarters in Tokyo. After a brief bow to the strength of local reservists' feelings on the matter, central headquarters late in 1935 cut off its attack on Minobe and compelled the local branches to do likewise. The 'conservative reaffirmation'[3] of the late 1930s began even before the February 26 (1936) rebellion, at least for the Military Reserve Association.

Mr. Shillony's article on the young officers who staged the February 26 Affair brings to light a fascinating set of implications which earlier writers have generally missed. His basic conclusion is that the rebel officers came closer to success than we have usually assumed. Indeed, their impressive contacts with persons in high places, and the hesitancy of top military authorities to label the

[2] See, for example, the discussion of the symbolic capabilities of political systems in Gabriel A. Almond and G. Bingham Powell, *Comparative Politics: A Developmental Approach* (Boston: Little, Brown, 1966), pp. 199–201 *et passim.*

[3] For a discussion of the 'conservative reaffirmation' that took place in the late 1930s, see *Sources of Japanese Tradition* (New York: Columbia University Press, 1964), II, 277–8 *et seq.*

officers and the men they commanded as a rebel force, suggest that for four days in February 1936 Japan stood poised at the brink of systemic political change from constitutional monarchy under the civil bureaucracy to direct rule by the military. That this change did not in fact occur takes nothing away from the seriousness of the threat. It was, perhaps, awareness of how near Japan had come to wholesale political change, rather than the victory of the army's 'Control faction' when the rebels were discredited, that encouraged both civil and military officials to pursue the conservative reaffirmation so steadfastly during the years that followed. The fear that when next a group of military rebels struck, the consequences might be even greater than those of February 1936 probably also contributed to the conservative ideological zeal marking the later 1930s.

Mr. Spaulding has given us an article that spans a longer period of time than the two discussed above. His topic, the 'new' or 'revisionist' bureaucrats, carries him from 1932 to the end of the Pacific War, although he also focuses on the mid-1930s. What comes out of this article most strongly is a sense of the growing importance of the union between civil and military bureaucrats as the 1930s progressed. Never revolutionary but always committed to promoting change, the new bureaucrats represented a growing interest in technocratic methods of building both the Japanese economy and the nation's warmaking capacity. For all their differences, the various factions of revisionist bureaucrats shared a common interest in efficiency, productivity, and the managerial approach to economic problems.

One conclusion which these articles seem to confirm is that the February 26 Affair, despite its near success, was not a major turning point in domestic or foreign policy. The conservative reaffirmation had begun to gather force before 1936, and the bureaucracy was not notably altered in personnel or attitudes after the rebellion; nor, as James Crowley has shown, was foreign policy and security thinking affected.[4] Of course, if Mr. Shillony is correct, the rebellion did come close to succeeding, and one could speculate that had it ushered in a period of direct military government, the results might well have involved significant modification of both domestic and foreign policy.

---

[4] James B. Crowley, *Japan's Quest for Autonomy: National Security and Foreign Policy, 1930–1938* (Princeton: Princeton University Press, 1966), pp. 246–9, 277–9.

But as it turned out the rebellion failed, the army did not take direct control, and basic policy lines did not change.

Another conclusion we can draw from these articles is that the political crises of the mid-1930s had their proximate causation in the internal rather than the external sphere, as I have contended in my final essay dealing briefly with the impact of Meiji Restoration history on the political thinking of the 1930s. The authors of this volume have figuratively put floodlights on the domestic locus of the sources that generated the principal political friction. To be sure, the concern of civilian as well as military officials with Japan's involvement in China and their fear of Russian land power and American sea power were factors in the politics of the time, but external problems were not the chief concern of the anti-Minobe reservist lobby, the young officers of the February Affair, or even the new bureaucrats. Their overriding motivation, in each case, was to correct the defects they perceived at home.

Finally, I would like to add some thoughts about where we may wish to go from here. The studies in this monograph represent an attempt to improve our understanding of the difficult politics of Japan in the 1930s. They verge also into social and intellectual history, for they are concerned with the social background and behavior of political actors and groups and with the ideas that inspired such behavior. At this stage of our research on recent Japanese history, it seems to me desirable to have achieved a new volume such as this, especially in view of the impressive array of previously untapped sources which the three main authors have brought to light. Yet what we lack is just as important as what we have. We are still particularly weak in doing social history, in the classic sense of expressing the character and quality of life of the people and exploring changes in social structure, institutions, and values.[5] We need to get beyond the political power elites and their satraps and enter into the realm of popular life and behavior (although there clearly remains room for important work on the social origins and education of the elites as well as of the common people).

This prescription applies not only to research on the 1930s, but also to our appraisal of the decades on either side of World War I. The

---

[5] For a trenchant summary of the development of social history, see *A Dictionary of the Social Sciences* (New York: Macmillan-Free Press, 1964), pp. 655–6.

twentieth century in Japan has brought rapid social change in almost every decade. One suspects, indeed, that the rapidity of change in living patterns during the early parts of this century had an important effect on the vicissitudes of politics, just as it has clearly had such an effect in the 1960s. Intelligent observation of the Japanese scene during the decade just past, taking into account the general prosperity, the impact of mass communications, and the burgeoning of Japan's mass culture, suggests answers to such political questions as why the Kōmeitō[6] appeals to certain social strata, why the Liberal Democrats have been obliged to build a new nationalistic emphasis into their policy lines, and why the formulas of doctrinaire socialism seem inapplicable to many of today's problems. May not the same kind of intelligent observation, accomplished through research into past sources, also be useful for understanding Taishō and prewar Shōwa history? Those of us working in this field ought to try harder to find out.

GEORGE M. WILSON

6 公明党

The Military Reserve
Association and the Minobe
Crisis of 1935

RICHARD J. SMETHURST

THE Imperial Military Reserve Association (Teikoku Zaigō Gunjinkai),[1] created in 1910 to spread military values to the general, non-military public, has become best known and gained its greatest notoriety as a political pressure group, especially in the year 1935 during the Minobe emperor-organ theory crisis. But, within the context of the organization's desire to be free from political involvement, this notoriety is ironic, for the leaders strove to adhere to the injunction of the *Imperial Rescript to Soldiers and Sailors*, which stated clearly that politics, which they defined as partisan politics, were taboo. Therefore, one must understand that my treatment here of the organization's participation in politics, especially in 1935, is a treatment of, not the norm, but an aberration in Zaigō Gunjinkai history.

This political involvement, albeit natural when viewed in the light of the organization's ideological and educational goals, was an aberration because much of the power which impelled the Zaigō Gunjinkai into politics, and all of the impetus which forced the organization into a more and more virulent attack on Professor Minobe Tatsukichi and his organ theory throughout 1935, came from below and within, not from above. It did not come from the central headquarters or even the army, as is often charged.[2] The Reserve Association became involved politically in the Minobe affair because, under the impetus of changing conditions and attitudes in the first half of what was to be the last prewar decade, groups and individuals advocating virulently nationalistic and xenophobic policies were

---

[1] 帝国在郷軍人会
[2] Hugh Byas, *Government by Assassination* (New York: Alfred A. Knopf, 1942), pp. 270–6, was one of the first to make the charge that the army sponsored the 1935 affair.

A

successful in gradually infiltrating the Zaigō Gunjinkai's local leadership. This activity centered around reserve officers who infiltrated the key positions in many of the eight hundred or more city- and county-based consolidated branches *(rengō bunkai)*,[3] the second lowest of the five levels of units within the organization's chain of command. Unlike the top three levels, commanded and staffed by both active and nonactive officers, the lower two levels, this one and the village- and town-based branches, were controlled by reservists only, men who were therefore eligible for, and often concurrently active in, two radical political and strictly reserve-officer groups, the Enlightened Ethical Association (Meirinkai) and the 36-Club (San-roku Kurabu).[4] (The latter organization was so extremist it even defended Lieutenant Colonel Aizawa Saburō, the assassin of Nagata Tetsuzan in August 1935, when General Suzuki Sōroku, national chairman of the Zaigō Gunjinkai, publicly condemned Aizawa.[5])

These men wanted to pressure the government to accept their radical political goals, that is, increased emphasis on the sacredness of Japan's emperor-centered polity, the establishment of one truly national political party free from partisan advantage, the protection of Japan and Asia from European and American imperialism, the purification of the intellectual community which fawned on Western systems of thought, the freeing of the military from all control but the emperor's, that is, freedom from all control, and in 1935, complete elimination from government of not only Minobe, his theories and supporters, but also of anything which they considered tainted with foreignism. These men infiltrated the larger 14,000-branch, three-

---

3 連合分会
4 明倫会, 三六クラブ
5 相沢三郎, 永田鉄山, 鈴木荘六. For discussions of these two organizations, see *Meirinkai kaishi* (A history of the Enlightened Ethical Society; Tokyo: Meirinkai Kaishi Henshūjo 明倫会会史編集所, 1942); *Shōwa jūnenchū ni okeru shakai undō jōkyō* 昭和十年中における社会運動状況 (The circumstances of social movements in 1935; Tokyo: Naimushō Keihokyoku 内務省警保局, 1937), originally a classified document published by the Home Ministry, pp. 195–212, 408–16; Kinoshita Hanji

木下半治, *Nihon fuashizumu shi* 日本ファシズム史 (A history of Japanese fascism; Tokyo: Iwasaki Shoten, 1949–51), II, 139–45. For the attitudes concerning Aizawa, see a Suzuki speech in *Sen'yū* 戦友 (Comrades in arms), the Reserve Association's main periodical, No. 304 (1935), 17, and Takahashi Masae 高橋正衛 and Imai Seiichi 今井清一, eds., *Gendaishi shiryō* 現代史資料 (Materials on contemporary Japanese history; Tokyo: Misuzu Shobō, 1962–), IV (*Kokkashugi undō I* 国家主義運動 [The nationalist movement, I]), 163.

million-member Zaigō Gunjinkai to increase their political leverage since their own organizations were smaller and weaker, and forced the central headquarters to take a stronger and stronger stand in the attack on the organ theory.[6] This action in turn forced the service ministries, the government, and even Professor Minobe himself to accept more and more radical solutions to the problem as the 1935 crisis progressed. The lower-level activity finally not only led to a breakdown in central control, but also motivated the Tokyo leadership of the Reserve Association to reestablish discipline over local units and to withdraw the organization from all political activity in October 1935, over four months before army leadership attained the same goal by suppressing the famed February 26 uprising.

One may wonder why, if the Zaigō Gunjinkai's central leadership reasserted its control over the organization in October 1935, it moved to a more radical attack on Minobe and did not crack down on dissidents earlier in the year when the problem first arose. The answer to this question lies partly in the fact that while General Suzuki and his subordinates did not want to initiate an attack on Minobe themselves, they still sympathized with many of the goals of the movement. Suzuki certainly agreed with the extremists' earliest demand, that the teaching and publication of the Tokyo University professor's theories be prohibited, and the general even approved of other progressively more radical demands, such as that Minobe resign from all government posts, that all political-party influence in government circles be eliminated, that the professor be indicted and tried for lese majesty, and that all of those who defended his teachings be eliminated from government. But once these goals had been at least partially attained and, ominously, when the 36-Club type of radicals began to call for the overthrow of the Okada[7] cabinet and the punishment of various political elder statesmen like Prince Saionji, and finally to criticize the War Ministry and Reserve Association for their 'weakness' in pressing for the attainment of these goals, then Suzuki and his headquarters subordinates reasserted

---

[6] *Shōwa jūnenchū*, pp. 196, 209–10. The 36-Club added one more goal, not pursued by the Meirinkai, to its list of aims: it declared its sympathy with the plight of Japan's economically embattled farmers. While the 36-Club's founding statement of December 1933 expressed this sympathy, thus revealing its position to be closer than the Meirinkai's to that of some of the army's radical young officers, the club offered no plan of action to aid rural Japan.

[7] Okada Keisuke 岡田啓介

firm discipline and withdrew the Zaigō Gunjinkai from politics.

The crisis in question originated with an attack in the Diet in February 1935 by two non-Zaigō Gunjinkai retired major generals, Etō Genkurō and Kikuchi Takeo.[8] They attacked Professor Minobe's scholarly interpretation of the Meiji Constitution, a document which if literally interpreted left no room for meaningful party government. According to the professor's explanation, the emperor was an organ (*kikan*)[9] of the state, rather than the state itself. Minobe never committed himself to saying that the emperor was not sovereign; instead he devised a means of limiting the power of the emperor and making the cabinet responsible to both the imperial person and the parliament, and hence, the electorate. The emperor and the people made up the nation, and the cabinet was delegated the task of revealing the emperor's will to the nation on the one hand, and the wishes of the populace to the ruler on the other. In other words, with this interpretation, while the Meiji Constitution's dictum of imperial sovereignty was not rejected, the civil government and the electorate gained importance and responsibility. Minobe's thesis limited the military also by restricting the independence of the army and navy from civil control to wartime and internal military matters, and by positing that budgetary affairs, decisions of war and peace, and foreign policy were strictly civilian governmental affairs. It was this last aspect, in addition to the alleged foreign origin of the theory and the use of the word *kikan*, generally used to denote machinery and subordinate parts of organizations, that particularly infuriated Etō, Kikuchi, and the rest of Minobe's opponents.[10]

In early March the Seiyūkai[11] and the reservists at the local level joined Minobe's parliamentary critics in the attack on the emperor-organ theory. While the political party entered the fray largely because its leaders saw an opportunity to throw the Okada government out of power and to regain the predominant position they had lost after the assassination of Prime Minister Inukai[12] in 1932, the reservists began their involvement on the local level, not the central one, and it was from below that the major impetus to action in 1935 continued to come.

---

8 江藤元九郎, 菊地武雄
9 機関
10 Frank O. Miller, *Minobe Tatsu-kichi: Interpreter of Constitutionalism in* *Japan* (Berkeley: University of California Press, 1965), Chaps. III, IV, V.
11 政友会
12 犬養毅

There is much evidence to support the contention that the Reserve Association was pressured by radicals in subordinate units to begin and to prosecute a vigorous campaign against the organ theory. First and foremost, as we shall see, throughout the crisis local reserve headquarters, particularly at the consolidated branch level, flooded the central headquarters, army, and cabinet with demands for more radical action. In March itself, local units in Nagano and Ishikawa Prefectures, and all over western Honshū and Kyūshū, held meetings, passed resolutions, and dispatched petitions, telegrams, and even delegations to Tokyo to pressure the government.[13] A typical resolution is this one written by the Reserve Association district commander in Hamada, and signed by the leaders of twenty-three local reserve branches. It was sent to Tokyo in early March:

> It is our intention to destroy completely Minobe's constitutional heresy and root out all subversive groups and theories that are in collusion with him.
>
>   We worship the great spirit of the imperial founding and pledge to unify our eternal and unparalleled imperial nation.[14]

Second, activists with extreme anti-*kikansetsu* views led many of these local Zaigō Gunjinkai headquarters, including the one in Hamada.[15] For example, thirteen *rengō bunkai* leaders were concurrently among the top thirty-five 36-Club leaders, and a number of others served in the club's central offices.[16] Existing evidence reveals leadership lists for 36-Club ties with the Zaigō Gunjinkai at the club's top level only; therefore, it is safe to assume that since over one-third of the radical group's officials served the Reserve

---

[13] *Shōwa jūnenchū*, pp. 211–12; *Selected Archives of the Japanese Army, Navy and Other Government Agencies, 1868–1945: Han-Minobe undō no gaikyō oyobi kanren shorui* 反美濃部運動の概況およ び関連書類 (An overview and documents related to the anti-Minobe movement), T1525–R224—96771, 96774, 96807, 96808, 96810, 96849–96852, 96900, 96901; Tamazawa Kōzaburō, 玉沢光三郎, *Shisō kenkyū shiryō* 思想研 究資料 (Materials for the study of thought), LXII (*Iwayuru tennō kikansetsu o keiki to suru kokutai meichō undō* 所謂

天皇機関説を契機とする国体明徴運動 [The movement for clarification of the national polity as instigated by the so-called emperor-organ theory crisis; Tokyo: Shihōshō Keijikyoku, 1940]), 129.

[14] *Han-Minobe undō*, R224—96807.

[15] 機関説, 浜田

[16] *Shōwa jūnenchū*, pp. 211–16; *Rikukaigun gunji nenkan* 陸海軍軍事年鑑 (Army and navy military yearbook; Tokyo: Gunjin Kaikan Shuppanbu, 1936), pp. 565–6.

Association, lower-ranking retired officers in the club must have served in both groups also.

Although the Meirinkai was a larger, more diffuse and less radical extremist group, a number of its members also influenced the Zaigō Gunjinkai to take stronger action in the Minobe affair. The activities of Lieutenant General Okudaira Shunzō, Meirinkai member and key leader in the Tokyo Azabu Ward reserve association, again in a consolidated branch, is one example.[17] Okudaira was active throughout 1935 in using the Azabu reservists to pressure General Suzuki and his headquarters, was one of the first reservist officials to call for the overthrow of the Okada government, and was the last to acquiesce to Suzuki's orders to cease radical activity; as late as December 8, Okudaira sponsored an anti-*kikansetsu*, anti-Okada-government meeting in Tokyo.[18] Moreover, there were a number of extremist activists in reservist local leadership positions for whom no evidence of 36-Club or Meirinkai membership exists; Saigō Tsugunori, a retired colonel, for example, was the head of the Tokyo Meguro Ward reserve association consolidated headquarters and an anti-Minobe extremist who, if he was not in one of the two radical groups, as seems likely, was at least in sympathy with their goals.[19]

Third, at least fifteen of the forty-three men who vowed in October not to leave Tokyo until the 'national polity' was 'clarified', that is, the organ theory problem was solved to their liking, and at least twelve of the twenty-two men in this group who called on Prime Minister Okada, as we shall see, on October 13, to present their radical demands, were local, not national, reservist leaders.[20] Fourth, on innumerable occasions, extremists in both of the two clubs mentioned above and other organizations including the Diet, men like Generals Ōi Narimoto,[21] Kikuchi, Etō, Okudaira, and Colonel Kobayashi Jun'ichirō,[22] driving force behind the 36-Club, made anti-organ-theory speeches to reservist consolidated-branch meetings. The repeated articles in regional newspapers reporting these

17 奥平俊蔵, 麻布
18 *Shōwa jūnenchū*, pp. 201, 410, 439.
19 西郷従徳, 目黒
20 *Tennō kikansetsu mondai ni kanshi Okada kaigun taishō (shushō) to no kondan jōkyō hōkoku* 天皇機関説問題に関し岡田海軍大将(首相)との懇談状況報告 (Report of our talk with Admiral Prime Minister Okada concerning the emperor-organ theory problem; Tokyo: Zaigō Gunjin Yūshi, 1935), pp. 1–4. *Nippon oyobi Nipponjin* 日本及日本人 (Japan and the Japanese), No. 331 (1935), 48–53.
21 大井成元
22 小林順一郎

gatherings reveal that the men who attended these affairs were invariably the *rengō bunkai* leaders and the key reservist and civil figures from the towns and villages in their local jurisdictions. Most of the fourteen former reservist officials in Aichi, Yamanashi, and Tokyo Prefecture branches interviewed in Japan by the author in the summer of 1969, moveover, indicated that they had attended such meetings. Conversely, however, there is no record of the Zaigō Gunjinkai's central leadership ever making such speeches.[23] Fifth, all fourteen men interviewed stated that political action in their areas was always initiated by the county-based consolidated-branch leaders.

In early March, this radically inspired local pressure began and increased, but the central headquarters, like the War Ministry itself, was cautious and attempted to head off this activism. General Suzuki feared involvement in partisan political affairs. The attacks of these local leaders were so vehement, however, that by mid-March Suzuki and his managing director, Akai Shunkai,[24] were compelled to take a cautious anti-Minobe stand. On March 12, Akai issued a circular to all district commanders for transmission to local leaders requesting that they educate their members in the dangers of Minobe's theory, but at the same time asking them to refrain from criticizing Minobe personally, from becoming involved in political battles, and from attacking Minobe and his theory in the name of the Reserve Association.[25] Many local leaders, to circumvent this directive, set up Reserve Association sympathizer groups (*dōshikai*)[26] to send out propaganda under a name different from, but similar to that of the Zaigō Gunjinkai. Of course, this move displeased central officials, but they did nothing to suppress it.

Suzuki again showed the cautious bent of central headquarters on March 14, when the Reserve Association's central council (*hyōgi-kai*)[27] met in Tokyo. Members, largely retired officers who served in consolidated-branch headquarters, like Ibuki Gengorō,[28] a Nagasaki reservist and 36-Club leader, and Saigō Tsugunori, pressed for an outright attack on Minobe and his sympathizers in official posts,

23 The references to such lectures in local newspapers are too frequent to cite here. For examples, see Tamazawa, pp. 153–66, and footnotes 41 and 48 below.

24 赤井春海
25 *Han-Minobe undō*, R224—96774.
26 同志会
27 評議会
28 伊吹元五郎

but Suzuki allowed the council to do no more than appoint an investigatory committee and publish a lukewarm condemnation of Minobe's theory, without mention of the professor's name.[29] The declaration which was sent out to all local branches read as follows:

> The emperor-organ theory is contrary to the essence of our unparalleled national polity and blasphemes the sacredness of the throne. It is absolutely incompatible with our traditional way of thinking. We must warn all Japanese to avoid involvement with this academic theory, to strive to bring about a greater respect for our constitution, to clarify the concept of our national polity, to exalt the Japanese spirit and to strive for all these goals loyally and sincerely.[30]

Unlike the declarations flooding central headquarters from all over Japan, this statement and the earlier circular were very mild at most. When one considers that Harada Kumao[31] and Prince Saionji viewed the instigation of the affair as an attempt by Baron Hiranuma Kiichirō to oust Ichiki Kitokurō,[32] a 'Minobe-ite', as president of the Privy Council, and that many of the reservist council members affiliated with the 36-Club were close associates of Hiranuma as well as Etō and Kikuchi, it is amazing that General Suzuki was able to hold the line against pressures to attack Minobe and Ichiki by name. And yet, a beginning of national Reserve Association opposition had been made under pressure from below.[33]

---

[29] *Han-Minobe undō*, R224—96765; *Tōkyō asahi shimbun* 東京朝日新聞 (Tokyo Asahi Newspaper), March 17, 1935, p. 1; *Teikoku zaigō gunjinkai sanjūnenshi* 帝国在郷軍人会三十年史 (The thirty-year history of the Imperial Military Reserve Association; Tokyo: Teikoku Zaigō Gunjinkai Hombu, 1944), pp. 269–70; *Shōwa jūnenchū*, p. 404.

[30] *Han-Minobe undō*, R224—96899; *Tōkyō asahi shimbun*, March 17, 1935, p. 1; *Sanjūnenshi*, p. 271.

[31] 原田熊雄

[32] 平沼騏一郎, 一木喜徳郎

[33] Harada Kumao wrote that the Minobe affair was part of a conspiracy by Hiranuma Kiichirō, vice president of the Privy Council, to increase his own political power and more particularly to take over Ichiki Kitokurō's post as president by accusing Ichiki of being a Minobe-ite. Since Hiranuma had contacts with Kikuchi, Etō, and many others among the extremists through various nationalist societies like the Kokuhonsha 国本社, this charge is plausible, especially when applied to the origins of the movement. However, even if Kikuchi and Etō opened their attacks on Minobe under Hiranuma's influence, once the movement was in motion it is very unlikely that the hundreds of persons involved acted out of a desire to further the political career of Hiranuma. Moreover, Harada's charge is undocumented and merely the supposition of an observer, albeit an astute one, of the 1935 scene. When Ichiki finally resigned in March*

Except for the brief abatement in radical activity during the visit of Emperor Pu-Yi of Manchuria to Japan, throughout the spring the activities of politicians, members of nationalistic societies, and local reservists became more and more frenzied, and Tokyo was flooded with resolutions, telegrams, and delegations from local reservist headquarters. For example, on March 25, Nakahara Kinji[34] of Matsumoto City led over 100 uniformed reservists who were concurrently members of the Nagano Prefecture Reserve Association Sympathizers' Society (Shinshū Gōgun Dōshikai)[35] to Tokyo in an effort to eliminate the influence of the organ theory and to oust Minobe from all of his governmental posts. The visitors first met with General Suzuki at reservist headquarters where they were told, rather ambiguously but not negatively, 'carry out your duties as soldiers and strive to break through our national dangers.' The Nagano reservists then visited Yasukuni and Meiji Shrines; at the shrine dedicated to the first modern emperor, they burned a complete set of the works of Professor Minobe, making at the same time the following proclamation:

> A non-Japanese, blasphemous, Europe-worshipping ideology which ignores our three-thousand-year-old tradition and ideals is rife. This liberalism which threatens to turn us into Western barbarians (*yōi*)[36] is basic to Minobe's beliefs. His books must be burned to show how we (reservists) feel about his servile individualism.[37]

Nakahara and three others of the Shinshū delegation remained in the capital to visit various cabinet members with copies of the proclamation.

Nakahara and his colleagues did not stop with this action. They planned a series of organized visits to all the shrines in Nagano Prefecture on May 27, Navy Day, so that the participants could pray for the 'clarification of the national polity'. In organizing this affair,

1936, he was replaced by Hiranuma. Harada Kumao, *Saionji kō to seikyoku* 西園寺公と政局 (Prince Saionji and the political situation; Tokyo: Iwanami Shoten, 1950–6), IV, 204, 217–18, 340–1. One should keep in mind, at the same time, that the Reserve Association had a long history of opposition to Minobe's theory. As far back as the April and May 1912 issues of *Sen'yū*, two anti-organ theory articles appeared, written by Hozumi Yatsuka 穂積八束, Minobe's leading academic opponent at the time.

34 中原謹司
35 信州郷軍同志会
36 洋夷
37 *Shōwa jūnenchū*, pp. 417–19.

they petitioned for support from the prefectural education committee, the shrine cooperative society, the prefectural mayors' association, the commanding officer of the army's Matsumoto regimental area, and other prefectural officials, and were turned down in every case. The only group willing to underwrite the effort was the Matsumoto Zaigō Gunjinkai district *(shibu)*[38] headquarters, largely because Nakahara himself and many of his associates were active reservist leaders in the area. Because of this, 66,000 prefectural reservists gathered at shrines and schools all over the prefecture. Ironically many of those participating in the ceremonies were local community leaders, with school children and other villagers. Ostensibly they came to pray, but in reality to pressure the government and reserve headquarters to take a less cautious attitude concerning the *kikan-setsu* problem.[39] Simultaneous to this kind of pressure on the government and Suzuki's headquarters, lectures by 36-Club and Meirinkai members, and all of the most active anti-Minobe leaders in the Diet, Kikuchi, Etō, Inoue Seijun,[40] and Ōi, were being given throughout the country to reservist gatherings, especially after the parliament had adjourned in April.[41] Thus even with the brief abatement in pressure during the imperial visit in April, efforts to maintain and even increase the intensity of the anti-Minobe feeling through lectures, meetings, resolutions, telegrams, and delegations to Tokyo continued throughout April, May, June, and July of 1935. Under this pressure, the Seiyūkai presented, and the Lower House of the Diet passed unanimously on March 26, a resolution attacking the organ theory, and on March 30 the cabinet council announced a decision to instruct the War, Navy, and Home Ministries to take appropriate measures in suppressing Minobe's writings.[42]

Under this same radical pressure, the Reserve Association too became more deeply involved in the attack on the organ theory. On April 25, the Zaigō Gunjinkai published a pamphlet by Yamashita

---

38 支部

39 *Shōwa jūnenchū*, p. 418.

40 井上清純

41 Tamazawa, pp. 153–66; *Shōwa jūnenchū*, pp. 417–18; *Tokushima nichi-nichi shimbun* 徳島日日新聞 (Tokushima daily newspaper), April 1, 1935, p. 2; *Fukuoka nichinichi shimbun* 福岡日日新聞 (Fukuoka daily newspaper), April 12, 1935, p. 1; April 13, p. 1; April

15, p. 3; April 22, p. 7; July 12, p. 4; July 15, p. 5; *Yamagata shimbun* 山形新聞 (Yamagata newspaper), May 31, 1935, p. 1.

42 Miller, pp. 227–8; Maruyama Masao, *Gendai seiji no shisō to kōdō* 現代政治の思想と行動 (Thought and action in modern politics; Tokyo: Miraisha, 1956–7), I, 62.

Tomobumi,[43] entitled *A View Concerning the Interpretation of the Greater Japan Imperial Constitution (Dai Nihon teikoku kempō no kaishaku ni kansuru kenkai)*,[44] which outlined his views, along with those of many other military men, on the imperial constitution and Professor Minobe's interpretation. It held that the Japanese constitution was based on an ancient tradition of divinely inspired imperial rule which could not be interpreted out of the constitution by any 'narrow or legalistic' approach. In other words, the emperor ruled as well as reigned and his sovereignty was indivisible. Political parties, politicians, and the emperor's other 'liberal' advisers, the pamphlet asserted, had discredited themselves by adhering to theories which created a duality between emperor and nation, an inevitable consequence of their being politicians and hence partisan. Only those who believed in the emperor as the state and served him by rising above partisanship were capable of advising the sovereign and ruling in his name. To create a truly great Japan, Yamashita believed, every citizen should be taught to believe in the true Japanese military spirit *(gunjin seishin)*[45] and to realize that opposing theories must be destroyed.[46]

The publication of a document of this sort was not out of line with the long-standing purpose of the Zaigō Gunjinkai and also revealed the anti-*kikansetsu* views of Suzuki and his headquarters colleagues; nevertheless, it is unlikely that it would have been published if there had been no pressure from below. The organization's leaders, since its inception in 1910, had advocated the dissemination to the non-military public of the very ideals which Yamashita expounded, and had long believed, like the author, that all other ideologies and types of political activity were subversive. They were so because by definition any concept or partisan action which created a duality between emperor and nation could not be orthodox or even Japanese. Thus, even though 100,000 copies of the pamphlet were distributed to active and retired officers and reserve branches all over Japan, men like Suzuki and Yamashita did not believe that they themselves were involved in political activities. Political activity, by their definition, included only partisan activity in the name of a party or 'foreign' ideology, not activity in the name of the emperor and for the

---

43 山下奉文
44 大日本帝国憲法の解釈に関する見解
45 軍人精神

46 Tamazawa, pp. 151–2; *Tōkyō asahi shimbun*, April 24, 1935, p. 2.

good of the whole nation. Because of this view, Yamashita's pamphlet, even while attacking the organ theory and other systems of thought which challenged the military's belief in a divine and ruling emperor, did not mention the need to eliminate from government Minobe, Ichiki, Okada, Saionji, and the other targets of the 36-Club and Meirinkai, that is, men who believed in, or did not repudiate publicly, these objectionable theories. That would have been an attack on individuals, partisan, and therefore political.[47]

Central headquarters maintained this 'conservative' approach throughout the early summer of 1935, despite pressure to the contrary from many local branch leaders. As the pressure from below continued, however, General Suzuki and his headquarters colleagues were gradually driven toward a more radical position, especially as lectures given to local reservist gatherings by 36-Club extremists began to stir up more and more opposition to Minobe and his associates.[48]

Thus, in mid-July, Suzuki and Vice-Chairman Admiral Nakano Naoe visited War Minister Hayashi Senjūrō[49] to inform him that the Zaigō Gunjinkai had decided to call a national conference for the purpose of attaining a 'final solution to the organ-theory affair'. The conference, destined to be a turning point, was scheduled for the end of the following month.[50]

Before the reservist national meeting was held, however, two events took place which complicated the issues and intensified Zaigō Gunjinkai reactions. First, on August 3, Prime Minister Okada, under strong pressure from the army, Reserve Association, Seiyūkai, and extremist groups, published after a month of intensive cabinet deliberations a governmental proclamation on the subject of the 'clarification of the national polity' and upheld the position that belief in the emperor as an organ of the state contradicted the basic principles of Japan's national polity.[51] But Okada's attempt at

---

[47] Tamazawa, pp. 164–5.

[48] *Shōwa jūnenchū*, pp. 207, 357.

[49] 中野直枝, 林銑十郎

[50] *Tōkyō asahi shimbun*, July 10, 1935, p. 2.

[51] 'Clarification of the national polity' (*kokutai meichō*) 国体明徴 was a very ambiguous term which came to mean different things to the various people and groups involved in the movement. Es-

sentially, however, it represented the goal of those who wanted to reestablish 'imperial rule', that is, wanted to replace the men who ruled Japan prior to 1930, mainly bureaucrats, party politicians, conservative military men, and other 'establishment' figures like Saionji, Nagata, Okada, Inukai, *et alii*, with themselves. Thus, *kokutai meichō* to the extremists came to be the goal of the so-*

mollifying Minobe's critics backfired; the extremists found the statement completely inadequate because Okada neglected to refer to the mystical union between emperor and nation in which most military men believed, because he did not mention Minobe or his theory by name or criticize the other targets of the attackers, Ichiki and Kanamori Tokujirō,[52] chief of the cabinet's legislative branch, and because he defended them in a separate statement published at the same time.[53] General Ōi found the statement so unsatisfactory that he questioned, only half facetiously, whether Minobe had not written the proclamation himself.[54] Second, the emotions of the most vociferous opponents of Professor Minobe's theory were intensified by the ousting in July of General Mazaki Jinzaburō,[55] the inspector general of military education, a hero to the radical right. Even General Suzuki, a more moderate critic of Minobe, was aggravated by Okada's failure to condemn the theory outright and by his public defense of Ichiki and Kanamori. Moreover, although Suzuki was not disappointed to see Mazaki go, one can imagine the chagrin with which he greeted the appointment of Watanabe Jōtarō,[56] the one ranking army officer who had defended the organ theory in public, as Mazaki's replacement. It was against this background of intensified pressure from below and even reserve headquarters' discontent that the Zaigō Gunjinkai's national conference convened in late August.[57]

Four-thousand five-hundred active officers and reservists, including War Minister Hayashi, his successor, Kawashima Yoshiyuki,[58] Navy Minister Ōsumi,[59] Generals Mazaki, Araki,[60] and Ōi, gathered at the Soldiers' Hall (Gunjin Kaikan)[61] in Tokyo on August 27 to

---

*called Shōwa restoration, a second renovation of government which would place radical civil and military types like Hiranuma and Mazaki in power rather than the conservatives already there. Hayashi, Kawashima, and Suzuki, being members of the 'power elite', held a view of *kokutai meichō* which was much less radical than that of the extremists.

52 金森徳次郎

53 Miller, pp. 234–8; *Fukuoka nichinichi shimbun*, August 22, 1935, p. 5; *Chūgoku mimpō* 中国民報 (Chūgoku newspaper), August 12, 1935, p. 2.

54 Ōi Narimoto, 'Shin rikushō ni

nozomu' (A request for a new war minister), *Nippon oyobi Nipponjin*, No. 329 (1935), 14–17.

55 真崎甚三郎

56 渡辺錠太郎

57 James B. Crowley, *Japan's Quest for Autonomy: National Security and Foreign Policy, 1930–1938* (Princeton: Princeton University Press, 1966), pp. 260–1.

58 川島義之

59 Ōsumi Mineo 大角岑生

60 Araki Sadao 荒木貞夫

61 軍人会館

attack what they felt was the government's equivocal position on the organ theory and its refusal to 'clarify the national polity'.[62] Suzuki's speech to the assembly revealed the change which had come about in the attitude of the reserve group's central headquarters toward this problem. He began by attacking the organ theory, individualism, liberalism, and all other 'foreign' ideologies which threatened Japan's 'sacred and traditional imperial polity' in the mid-1930s. While those Japanese, he said, who rejected the traditional virtues of 'obedience, respect, love for the emperor, and virility' and accepted the foreign values of 'freedom, indolence, and hedonism on which the organ theory is based' were only a small part of the Japanese citizenry, the very fact that even one Japanese preached these dissolute ideals was a threat to the true Japanese polity. Suzuki demanded that all of these values and all people who believed in them be rooted out of responsible positions before the nation collapsed, a fate which had to be especially guarded against because of the equally dangerous threat of foreign military 'imperialism'. Suzuki believed, in other words, that just as Japan was facing Western military might, European and American intellectual values were like a 'fifth column', undermining from within Japan's will to resist. In the light of these threats, he felt that the August 3 government proclamation was inadequate in not stating that the emperor alone was sovereign, and for not touching on the need to eliminate all of Minobe's followers from responsible positions.

With this speech, Suzuki disclosed that central headquarters was advocating a practice which it had avoided and warned against for the previous six months, that it now favored attacks on individuals, even if not as yet by name. Moreover, as he went on to speak about election reform, Suzuki revealed his organization's deeper involvement in politics. He asked reservists to vote in the forthcoming elections not for party politicians who only worried about partisan or local district advantage, but for candidates who worked for the national and imperial good *(tengyō no yokusansha)*.[63] Needless to say, Suzuki insisted that he was not becoming political; he could justify this recommendation by saying that he supported those who strove to fulfil the imperial work and thus were not partisan. Nevertheless, his speech represented the most extreme political

[62] *Tōkyō asahi shimbun*, August 28, 1935, p. 1.

[63] 天業の翼賛者

pronouncement of the reserve headquarters, for never before had a chairman instructed his members publicly on how to vote.[64]

For the first time in the year-long crisis, the national reserve group criticized the government directly. After Suzuki's speech, the assembled members unanimously passed a resolution which was as usual published in the name of all three million members and represented the high point in Reserve Association opposition to the organ theory. It read as follows:

1 The emperor is sovereign and is Japan's glory. We believe this absolutely.
2 The organ theory blasphemes the emperor, endangers the principle of supreme command, and threatens to destroy our national polity. It must be destroyed completely. Moreover, any government proclamations which clarify national sovereignty contrary to our expectations must not be tolerated.
3 Under present world conditions, national defense is our greatest duty and we members must root out pacifism and anti-war ideas and strive loyally and sincerely to improve our national defenses.
4 The conducting of honest elections is one of the highest responsibilities of the populace. We reservists must use our voting rights correctly, become loyal examples and elect candidates who support the imperial duty.[65]

During the three months after the meeting, the war minister and reserve leaders all over Japan called time and again for the government to take a stand similar to that proposed in the Zaigo Gunjinkai resolution. But at the same time, one should bear in mind that the demands this placed on the government are difficult to define, for the meaning of the declaration was interpreted differently by the various individuals and groups involved.

It is difficult to assess the impact of this conference on the government and its policies toward Professor Minobe and his theory. On the one hand, by Prime Minister Okada's own admission, he declined Suzuki's invitation to attend the meeting because he feared Reserve

---

[64] Suzuki speech of August 27, 1935, as reported in *Sen'yū*, No. 304 (1935), 14–17.

[65] *Tōkyō asahi shimbun*, August 28, 1935, p. 1; *Sen'yū*, No. 304 (1935), 17.

Association pressure.[66] Instead he sent his cabinet secretary to make an innocuous statement about how well the Reserve Association had served the nation in the past.[67] Home Minister Gotō Fumio,[68] moreover, remarked that the strong Zaigō Gunjinkai stand of August 27 was a bad omen in that it forboded increased reservist activity in the future. He was convinced that if some local branches were still not active before central headquarters entered the battle in full force, they certainly would be so now.[69]

On the other hand, the issue was noticeably intensified by Minobe himself, who gave the extremists fuel to add to the fire. The professor had been under investigation by the Justice Ministry from the time Etō Genkurō brought charges of lese majesty against him in February. On September 17, shortly after Minobe's family and friends, fearing for his health and safety, persuaded him to resign all of his official positions including his seat in the House of Peers, the office of the procurator-general informed him that the charges against him had been dropped. The Justice Ministry assumed that Minobe's resignation was an admission of error in his works. But, the next day, in announcing his resignation from the upper house, Minobe denied recantation and said he was resigning only because the atmosphere in the House of Peers made it difficult for him to carry out his duties successfully.[70] His statement destroyed all hope that Prime Minister Okada had of seeing the organ-theory issue die a natural death, for it, more than the activities of any pressure group, infuriated the extremists and heated the crisis to such a dangerous intensity that the government almost collapsed.

Minobe's declaration and the contradiction between it and the position of the justice minister began a new stage in the organ-theory controversy. Throughout September and October, petitions and telegrams poured into the government from radical groups and individuals all over Japan. The Zaigō Gunjinkai was no exception. Local branches held meetings and passed resolutions which were sent to Tokyo from every section of the nation. Within two days after Minobe's statement, consolidated branch headquarters such

66 Okada Keisuke, *Okada Keisuke kaikoroku* 岡田啓介回顧録 (Memoirs of Okada Keisuke; Tokyo: Mainichi Shimbunsha, 1950), pp. 118–19.

67 *Tōkyō asahi shimbun*, August 28,

1935, p. 1; *Sen'yū*, No. 304 (1935), 17.

68 後藤文夫

69 Harada, IV, 317–18.

70 Miller, p. 242.

as those in Yokosuka and Kumamoto were calling for a new indictment and a stiff jail sentence for Minobe as well as the overthrow of
the 'insincere' Okada government.[71] For example, during a meeting
in Okayama of all local reservist leaders and regular army officials
on October 10, vehement attacks were made against the government and Professor Minobe. The division commander there, Tatekawa Yoshitsugu,[72] a principal actor in the Manchurian drama of
1931, made a long and impassioned speech attacking the organ
theory and the government. This political involvement was surpris-
ing for an officer who had served many years as a strategic planner
on the General Staff, and it was a reflection of the changing attitude
even of high-ranking officers toward the *Imperial Rescript*'s ban on
political activity. After Tatekawa's speech, the gathering passed
a strong resolution criticizing the government and appointed a local
reserve official to present it to the prime minister in Tokyo. The
resolution read as follows:

> We (145,000 Okayama reservists) resolve that all theories
> and ideas which are contrary to the ideal of the great imperial
> Japanese sovereignty must be destroyed and the national
> polity clarified.
>
> The government should not be allowed to exist any longer,
> for it is insincere and does not intend to clarify the national
> polity.
>
> All persons who defend or believe in the organ theory
> should be dealt with resolutely and swept away.[73]

Other reserve units all over Japan took similar 'hard line' positions.

The reservist headquarters and the War Ministry also advanced
a new and more extreme attitude even though they maintained a
relatively more moderate position than many local-reservist leaders.
On the one hand, both Suzuki and Kawashima Yoshiyuki, the new
war minister, called for a strong government proclamation, and for
the first time for the indictment of Minobe and the ousting of Ichiki

---

[71] Tamazawa, pp. 206–8; *Kyūshū nichinichi shimbun* 九州日日新聞 (Kyūshū daily newspaper), September 25, 1935, p. 1; October 16, p. 1; October 17, p. 2; *Gōyū* 郷友 (Local friends), a Saga 佐賀 magazine, vi.10 (1935), 21; *Nagoya shimbun* 名古屋新聞 (Nagoya newspaper), October 6, 1935, p. 2; *Yamagata shimbun*, October 29, 1935, p. 3; November 17, p. 3; November 26, p. 3.

[72] 建川美次

[73] *Chūgoku mimpō*, October 12, 1935, p. 1.

and Kanamori, both of which were extremist demands; but on the other hand, neither man was adamant on these two issues. Moreover, Suzuki, unlike many of his local-reservist subordinates, did not call for the overthrow of the cabinet as a precondition to the government's acceptance of the reservist position; nevertheless, he was willing to admit that if the cabinet hesitated to meet reservist demands and then fell, he would have no regrets.[74] To attain its goals, central headquarters prosecuted a vigorous petition and visitation campaign in September and October of 1935. Thus, the Reserve Association had involved itself in partisanship and betrayed even its own definition of what was political.[75]

In spite of intense national-headquarters and local-reservist pressure, Prime Minister Okada hesitated to condemn important and respected members of his government and tried to take a stand which, although extreme as compared to his position of the past spring, was still moderate by 36-Club and the new Reserve Association standards. He told a press conference on September 18 that his view of the organ theory and the national polity was the same as that outlined in the August 27 reservist proclamation. Without question his interpretation of it differed even from Suzuki's.[76]

But, events had passed the prime minister by; his position fell not too far short of satisfying Suzuki and his headquarters, but it did not meet the demands of the 36-Club at all. In late September, therefore, 44 club-affiliated reserve officers, many of whom were local Zaigō Gunjinkai leaders, took the unprecedented step of converging on Tokyo to pressure the government. For several weeks these men, led by General Ōi and Colonel Kobayashi Jun'ichirō, head of the radical 36-Club, met with army, reserve, and civil officials and called upon the cabinet and prime minister either to meet all of their demands or resign.[77] On October 13, after vowing not to leave Tokyo until the problem was solved to their satisfaction, twenty-two of the men, fourteen of whom were Reserve Association leaders, called on the prime minister and presented him with a complete list of their demands. When he was not willing to accept many of them, the meeting broke up as Ōi, the group's spokesman, shouted for

---

74 *Shōwa jūnenchū*, p. 407.

75 Tamazawa, p. 206; *Nagoya shimbun*, October 10, 1935, p. 1.

76 *Tōkyō asahi shimbun*, September 19,

1935, p. 1.

77 Tamazawa, p. 194; *Shōwa jūnenchū*, pp. 411–12.

Okada's resignation and called him, a retired admiral, an insult to the honor of the military services and a 'wicked and worthless person'.[78] Two days later, under pressure from the War Ministry as well as the reservists, Prime Minister Okada made a second governmental statement on the organ theory and the 'clarification of the national polity'. He said that the emperor was sovereign and that any 'foreign' ideology which limited the imperial power or denied the emperor's complete sovereignty such as the 'so-called organ theory' had to be swept away. No ideal which ran counter to Japan's 'divine national polity', he stated, could be allowed to exist.[79]

Many extremist local leaders of the Reserve Association continued to find the prime minister's position 'weak' and inadequate, and, therefore, to hold meetings and dispatch petitions to Tokyo. Central headquarters decided that the government's public condemnation of the organ theory satisfied its demands, even though not all Zaigō Gunjinkai goals had been attained.[80] This change in policy took place because local reservists now began for the first time to criticize Suzuki and his staff officers, and to create a new specter, the fear of a complete breakdown of central control over the local activists. This caused consternation in the Kudanshita headquarters; it was, after all, a danger infinitely more frightening to them than the continued service in government of a few 'Minobe-ite' officials. Therefore, on October 21, all of the commanding generals of the Zaigō Gunjinkai's fourteen domestic consolidated districts met with central leaders in Tokyo and decided that discipline must be reasserted and that the second national conference, scheduled for the next day at the demand of local Tokyo subordinate leaders, should be cancelled. These central officers then passed a resolution which was dispatched to every branch of the association; it called for a halt to local activity, a severance of all connections with reserve officer organizations like the 36-Club, and continued education concerning Japan's true, non-foreign-tainted national polity.[81] The declaration read as follows:

[78] *Tennō kikansetsu mondai ni kanshi Okada*, pp. 1–33; *Nippon oyobi Nipponjin*, No. 331 (1935), 48–53.

[79] Miller, p. 246.

[80] Tamazawa, pp. 214, 218; *Kyūshū nichinichi shimbun*, October 21, 1935,

p. 3; *Tōkyō asahi shimbun*, October 22, 1935, p. 2.

[81] *Tōkyō asahi shimbun*, October 22, 1935, p. 2; *Saga shimbun* (Saga newspaper), October 23, 1935, p. 1.

1 Although there has been much debate since the publication of the second governmental proclamation, it generally follows the gist of the resolutions passed at the August 27 congress. Therefore, from now on, the Reserve Association will limit its activities to watching vigilantly the government's action.

2 Local headquarters should take appropriate steps to see that members receive more thorough information concerning the 'clarification of the national polity'.

3 We shall depend on the military ministers to deal with the problem from now on.

4 Reserve Association members and branches will not act in concert with other reservist organizations including those which have assumed names similar to its own (*zaigō gunjinkai dōshikai*) and we will inform the nation of this decision.[82]

Thus, on October 21, the Reserve Association called a halt to radical actions by its members, and on October 31 spelled out even more clearly its desire to end the political activities of local members. In the second statement, Suzuki warned members that advocating the overthrow of the cabinet was clearly a political activity and would not be tolerated.[83] The Reserve Association, after becoming entangled for a short time in partisan politics, now stepped back again and reinforced its internal discipline in late October, four months before army leaders did the same thing after the February 26, 1936 *coup d'état* attempt.

The events of 1935 marked a turning point in reservist history. Although for the first twenty years of the organization's existence, from 1910 to 1930, its leaders had striven to keep it free from political involvement, the Zaigō Gunjinkai became more and more deeply involved in the political wars, until by the late summer of 1935, Suzuki and his staff led the organization into a partisan conflict which even by the chairman's own definition had to be considered political. Needless to say, although Suzuki himself had a deep reverence for the emperor, an antipathy for Minobe's theory, and a long-standing mistrust of politicians, most of the reservist involvement had been

82 Tamazawa, pp. 219–20.   *jūnenchū*, pp. 364, 405.
83 Tamazawa, pp. 219–22; *Shōwa*

forced upon him and his headquarters by local extremist leadership. Moreover, while there is an abundance of evidence to show that the impetus for action came from below and from contacts between local reservist headquarters and radical political groups and while, as we have seen, the lower-level activity was always a step ahead of central headquarters and the army, there is no evidence to show that Suzuki and his colleagues in Kudanshita directed the anti-Minobe affair. If central headquarters had taken the lead, one would expect them to have sent out directives calling for reservist action. Yet, for example, twenty-three unpublished, loose-leaf volumes of local records, belonging to the former Anjō[84] Town (now City) branch in Aichi Prefecture, contain no orders, letters, directives, or other correspondence calling for local anti-*kikansetsu* action. In the 200 orders and instructions from higher headquarters between 1914 and 1944 found among these records, only five mention the 1935 movement even peripherally, and none can by any stretch of the imagination be called instructions to take political action.[85] Thus, because of the absence of evidence to show central headquarters and War Ministry control, because of the close ties between ultra-nationalist leaders and consolidated branch leaders, and because of the tremendous amount of lower-level activity which was always a step ahead of central headquarters' and the ministry's actions, I can only conclude that the main impetus for attacking the professor and his theory came not from the army above, but from local reservists below.

Certain beliefs and feelings, such as, for example, loyalty to emperor and nation, distrust of intellectuals and their theories, fear of civilian control of the military, antipathy toward political parties, motivated these activist consolidated branch officers, but these were feelings shared by military men at all levels of the army, navy, and Reserve Association, and thus do not explain why only the lower level of leadership acted vigorously.

The best explanation lies in a different realm: the background and training of these men. While the Tokyo officers shared all of their regional subordinates' dislike for Minobe's theory, they believed

---

84 安城

85 The documents, now stored in the Anjō City Public Library, were in the possession of Kuroyanagi Masao 畔柳 真爽雄, former chief of the city's Reserve Association branch, until the author interviewed him in July 1969.

the maintenance of discipline and control within the services and the Zaigō Gunjinkai to be more important. This difference in point of view was a direct consequence of their military education and background. Suzuki and most of his key subordinates were members of the small group of strategic planners who by virtue of their superior grades at the Military Academy and subsequent graduation from the War College had risen to hold, before retirement, the top posts in the army and navy (primarily the army). Most of the lower-ranking members of his staff, as active-duty field-grade officers with similar educations and staff positions in the ministries and general staffs, were future members of the same elite. In other words, the Zaigō Gunjinkai was directed at the central level by both the past and future elite of the army, men who by nature of their broad military education viewed the military's role in a larger political, economic, and diplomatic context, and who emphasized rational *overall* national planning and organization. These men naturally viewed discipline and control as very important.

Conversely, consolidated branch activists were a different breed altogether. While about half of the men who functioned in these posts in 1935 were lieutenants who had had only one or two years of active-service experience, the politically activist *rengō bunkai* officers were mostly retired low-ranking generals or field-grade career officers. These men, usually controlling urban consolidated branches, were former troop commanders, officers who had not attended the War College and were not part of the army's central elite. Thus, because they were educated to view the military services as the emperor's personal commands, because they believed the army and navy to be legally equal and morally superior to the civil government, and because they had not received a broad War College education, these men accepted the spiritual values associated with the emperor, the 'ethno-nationalistic' values, as more important even than the necessities of discipline and command.[86]

In addition to the differences in the ideology of these two groups,

---

[86] For discussions of this dichotomy in the imperial Japanese army, see Takahashi Masae, *Shōwa no gumbatsu* 昭和の軍閥 (The military clique in the Shōwa period; Tokyo: Chūō Kōronsha, 1969), pp. 13–26, and Crowley, pp. 83–91 *et passim*. A description of the different types of officers serving at various levels of command in the Reserve Association can be found in the author's Ph.D. dissertation, 'The Social Basis for Japanese Militarism: The Case of the Imperial Military Reserve Association' (University of Michigan, 1968), pp. 146–71.

and one must remember that the differences were relative, not absolute, General Furushō Motoo,[87] assistant war minister at the time, saw another motivation for the actions of the local leaders. Harada Kumao quotes Furushō as saying that the consolidated-branch leaders pressured headquarters and the army because they were bitter over being forced to retire before reaching general rank and over their resentment toward the preference given War College graduates within the army.[88] It was this dichotomy which provided the context for anti–Minobe political action, and it was the central elite which reasserted authority over its traditional subordinates in October 1935, over four months before an overlapping part of the same elite reasserted authority over another generation of these same subordinates after the February 26 incident.

General Suzuki and his army and navy associates did not stop at merely suppressing local reservist activity in later 1935. Suzuki, former chief of the army's General Staff, and a member of the army's elite, may have distrusted politicians and revered the emperor, but he also thought highly of discipline within the army as well as within his Reserve Association, especially since by late 1935 his major political goals, particularly the abandonment of party governments, had been achieved. Therefore, the Zaigō Gunjinkai headquarters, in conjunction with the two service ministries, revised the bylaws of the association in 1936 in order to bring it under direct army and navy control for the first time and in order to strengthen central headquarters' discipline over local branches. Because of this 1935 experience, no more local-level political activity was allowed between 1936 and the organization's demise in 1945.

[87] 古荘幹郎   [88] Harada, IV, 362.

The February 26 Affair:
Politics of a Military Insurrection

BEN-AMI SHILLONY

Introduction

THE February 26 Affair (*ni ni-roku jiken*) of 1936 has fascinated a great many Japanese and non-Japanese writers alike. One reason for this may be that the Affair contains all the ingredients of a successful kabuki drama: it has both pure-hearted heroes (the rebels or their victims, depending on the viewer's political standpoint) and sinister villains. The tension slowly rises and reaches its climax with an outburst of bloodshed against a snowy background. For a while, the whole stage is in confusion and tumult, as villains cross swords with heroes. Finally the wicked, or idealistic, rebels fail and the gracious, or misguided, emperor wins. The audience expects the losers to commit suicide, but, alas, most of them refuse and are executed. Everything is again well, or rotten, in the condition of Japan as the curtain goes down on the Affair.

But there was more to the Affair than its dramatic setting. It was the greatest and most serious attempt to carry out a *coup d'état* in twentieth-century Japan, paralyzing government for four days, endangering the lives of the whole power elite and shaking the foundations of the state as it had been constituted since the Meiji Restoration. The Affair was also followed by a thorough purge of the Japanese army and by a strengthening of the army's position *vis-à-vis* the civilian government.

The rebels themselves were easily identifiable. They were tried and executed together with some of their civilian collaborators. Many others, who had assisted them during the rebellion, were also tried and punished. But sources available to us now suggest that there was still more collusion with and support for the rebels than the court-martial preferred to admit. These additional connections between the rebels and certain groups within the establishment of

the time may provide a new dimension to the whole February 26
Affair.

The Rebels

Who were the 'insurgent officers' *(kekki shōkō)*[1] of the February
26 Affair? Contrary to what is often assumed, most of them did not
come from an economically deprived rural gentry, nor were they
embittered junior officers frustrated in their military careers. The
majority of them came from well-to-do urban families and their
career prospects were bright as long as they abstained from subversive activities.

Out of the 15 officers who were executed or who committed suicide
for leading the rebellion, more than half were sons of high-ranking
military figures. Captain Nonaka Shirō, the senior commander among
the rebels, was the son of Major General Nonaka Masaaki;[2] Lieutenant Kurihara Yasuhide was the eldest son of Colonel Kurihara
Isamu;[3] Captain Kōno Hisashi's father was Rear Admiral Kōno
Sakinta;[4] Lieutenant Nakahashi Motoaki's father was Major General
Tarui Akihira;[5] Lieutenant Takeshima Tsuguo was the eldest son of
Major General Takeshima Tōjirō;[6] Lieutenant Sakai Naoshi was
the son of Major General Sakai Heikichi;[7] Lieutenant Nibu Seichū's
father was Navy Captain Nibu Takehiko, his maternal grandfather
was the Meiji General Ōkubo Toshisada and another of his relatives
was Prime Minister Okada Keisuke;[8] Second Lieutenant Hayashi
Hachirō was the son of Major General Hayashi Daihachi, the
Commander of the 9th Infantry Regiment, who was killed in the
Shanghai Incident of 1932.[9] Captain Andō Teruzō was the son of
a Keio University professor.[10]

The military units to which they mainly belonged, the infantry
regiments of the First and the Imperial Guards Divisions, were

1 蹶起将校

2 野中四郎, 勝明. Kōno Tsukasa
河野司, ed., *Ni ni-roku jiken* 二・二六
事件 (Tokyo: Nihon Shūhōsha, 1957),
p. 366.

3 栗原安秀, 勇. Kōno, p. 379.

4 河野寿, 左金太. Kōno, p. 367.

5 中橋基明, 垂井明平. Kōno, p. 381.

6 竹島継夫, 藤次郎. Kōno, p. 375.

7 坂井直, 兵吉. Kōno, p. 384.

8 丹生誠忠, 猛彦, 大久保利貞, 岡田
啓介. Kōno, pp. 382–3; *Dai jimmei jiten*
大人名辞典 (Tokyo: Heibonsha, 1956),
I, 460.

9 林八郎, 大八, Kōno, p. 393; *Dai
jimmei jiten*, V, 214.

10 安藤輝三. Kōno, p. 371.

among the most prestigious units of the Japanese army and many sons of famous people, including the nobility, were assigned to them as officers. Stationed in the capital, these divisions enjoyed the status of being the emperor's guard, the advantages of being close to the army's central headquarters and the pleasures of city life.

Although not all of the rebel officers could eventually be admitted to the War College and join the army's elite, there is no evidence that their promotion was blocked by a hostile establishment. Quite the opposite, their good education and military background at home, as well as the right connections of their families, assured most of them of brilliant careers.[11] Muranaka Kōji, who was dismissed from the army together with Isobe Asaichi for political activities, had already been admitted to the War College.[12] Both he and Isobe were offered, after their dismissal, a large stipend for studying abroad, which they declined.[13]

The geographical background of the rebel officers reveals a high frequency of Kyūshū, or more exactly Saga, origin. Kōda Kiyosada,[14] Kurihara, Nakahashi, and Nakajima Kanji[15] were all from Saga; Kōno and Yasuda Masaru[16] were from Kumamoto; Nibu and Tanaka Masaru[17] were from Kagoshima. Nakahashi's great grandfather was Nakahashi Tōichirō, a participant in the Saga Rebellion of 1874.[18]

The Saga origin, no doubt, fostered the ideological connections between these officers and the leading Kōdō (Imperial Way)[19] generals, Mazaki Jinzaburō and Yanagawa Heisuke,[20] both Saga men and both former commanders of the First Division in Tokyo. But this was not their main link, for the rebel officers considered themselves part of a wider and amorphous young officers' movement, which stood for a national reform, embodied in the idea of a Shōwa restoration, and obtained much of its inspiration from Kita Ikki's[21] *A Plan for the Reorganization of Japan.*

By 1936 these officers were already seasoned plotters. They had

---

11 Lieutenant Takeshima, for instance, graduated from the Military Academy at the top of his class.

12 村中孝次, 磯部浅一. *Gendaishi shiryō* 現代史資料 (Tokyo: Misuzu Shobō, 1962–), IV (*Kokkashugi undō I* 国家主義運動 1), 145.

13 Oki Shūji 沖修二, *Yamashita Tomobumi* 山下奉文 (Tokyo: Yama-

shita Tomobumi Kinenkai, 1958), p. 220.

14 香田清貞

15 中島莞爾

16 安田優

17 田中勝

18 中橋藤一郎. Kōno, p. 381.

19 皇道

20 真崎甚三郎, 柳川平助

21 北一輝

been consulted by the high commanders who planned the abortive March and October 1931 coups and were even assigned a role in the latter.[22] In May 1932, they refused to participate in the plot conducted by young naval officers and civilian rightists, but the army cadets who participated in that affair were Muranaka's students from the Military Academy.[23] When Prime Minister Inukai was assassinated, Andō, Kurihara, and their comrades approached War Minister Araki and asked him to take over the government.[24]

In November 1933, some of Kurihara's former soldiers attempted a *coup d'état* in Saitama Prefecture.[25] In November 1934, Isobe and Muranaka were dismissed from active service for allegedly plotting a military insurrection.[26] The disclosure of that plot facilitated the removal, ten months later, of General Mazaki from the post of inspector general of military education. The inflammatory pamphlets of Isobe and Muranaka, following Mazaki's removal, led to the assassination of Major General Nagata Tetsuzan by Lieutenant Colonel Aizawa Saburō[27] and the final dismissal of Isobe and Muranaka from military service.

The leaders of the February 1936 rebellion were staunch supporters of the Kōdō faction in the army's central headquarters, which was gradually expelled from power by the war minister, General Hayashi Senjūrō.[28] But when Hayashi was obliged to resign in September 1935, following Nagata's assassination, the ouster of the Kōdō officers from key positions had not yet been fully accomplished: there was still a Kōdō group in the War Ministry, the most prominent member of which was Major General Yamashita Tomobumi,[29] head of the Research Bureau; moreover, the Kōdō faction was still powerful in the Tokyo area, where General Yanagawa commanded the First Division.[30]

---

[22] Isobe Asaichi 磯部浅一, 'Isobe Asaichi no gokuchū shuki 磯部浅一の獄中手記', *Bungei* 文藝, VI.3 (March 1967), 266. (This portion of Isobe's prison diary was published for the first time in that issue of *Bungei*.) See also *Gendaishi shiryō*, IV, 69.

[23] Kōno, p. 154; Hashikawa Bunzō 川橋文三, ed., *Chōkokkashugi* 超国家主義 (Tokyo: Chikuma Shobō, 1964), p. 416.

[24] Takamiya Tahei 高宮太平, *Gunkoku taiheiki* 軍国太平記 (Tokyo: Kan-

tōsha, 1951), p. 152.

[25] *Gendaishi shiryō*, IV, 134–5.

[26] *Gendaishi shiryō*, IV, 145–7.

[27] 永田鉄山, 相沢三郎

[28] 林銑十郎

[29] 山下奉文

[30] The information about the command of the Japanese military at that time is derived mainly from Hata Ikuhiko 秦郁彦, *Gun fuashizumu undō shi* 軍ファシズム運動史 (Tokyo: Kawade Shobō, 1962); Ōtani Keijirō 大谷敬二郎, *Ni**

The new war minister, Kawashima Yoshiyuki,[31] did not belong to either faction, but he appointed some Kōdō sympathizers to important positions: Major General Iwasa Rokurō[32] was made chief of the military police and Colonel Murakami Keisaku[33] was made head of the Military Affairs Section in the War Ministry. General Yanagawa was transferred to Taiwan, but a Kōdō man, General Kashii Kōhei,[34] was appointed as commander of the Tokyo garrison, which included the two Tokyo-based divisions. The new commander of the First Division, General Hori Takeo,[35] was a Kōdō sympathizer and so were some of his regimental commanders.

The Kōdō group in the Tokyo area planned to turn the forthcoming public court-martial of Lieutenant Colonel Aizawa into a stage for attacks on the army leadership and on the regime. The judges for the trial had been appointed by General Yanagawa and the counsels for the defense were a Kōdō officer, Lieutenant Colonel Mitsui Saki-chi,[36] and a rightist member of the House of Peers, Dr. Uzawa Sō-mei.[37]

The Tōsei (Control)[38] faction, which dominated the General Staff, decided to counter the possible repercussions of that trial on the Tokyo junior officers by transferring the whole First Division to Manchuria in March 1936 before the expected end of the trial.

This development put before the radical company commanders and their backers the choice either of acting soon or losing the chance to act for a long time. They preferred to act, notwithstanding the trial, but only after they had secured such support as would give them a chance of success.

Support from Above

The firmest support for the rebels was expected to come from the Kōdō senior officers in the Tokyo area, the War Ministry, and the Supreme War Council.

---

ni-roku jiken no nazo 二・二六事件の謎 (Tokyo: Kashiwa Shobō, 1967)—at the time of the rebellion Ōtani was commander of the military police in Chiba Prefecture; and *Nihon kindaishi jiten* (Tokyo: Tōyō Keizai Shimpōsha, 1958), pp. 720–6.

31 川島義之

32 岩佐禄郎
33 村上啓作
34 香椎浩平
35 堀丈夫
36 満井佐吉
37 鵜沢総明
38 統制

In September 1935, a few days after being appointed war minister, General Kawashima received Isobe Asaichi,[39] the chief instigator of the rebellion, who had been dismissed earlier for grave disciplinary reasons. According to Isobe's prison diary, the minister at that meeting praised Generals Araki Sadao and Mazaki Jinzaburō[40] and expressed his support for a national reform. Three months later, in December 1935, Isobe met with the vice minister of war, General Furushō Motoo,[41] and informed him that if things were not changed soon, there would be bloodshed. Major General Yamashita of the War Ministry also told Isobe bluntly: 'If you men wish to do something, the sooner you do it, the better.'[42]

On December 20, 1935, Isobe conferred with General Mazaki, then a member of the Supreme War Council. Mazaki agreed with Isobe's prediction that, if Japan were not reformed quickly, there would soon be bloodshed.[43] A week later, Captain Kōda was received by Mazaki and was told that the new inspector general of military education, General Watanabe Jōtarō (later killed by the February 26 rebels), should be removed from office.[44] In January 1936, Isobe was received by Colonel Murakami Keisaku of the War Ministry, who told him emphatically: 'Unless something happens very soon, chances are that the old problems will not be solved.'[45]

The hint was clear, as was the moral support. Isobe therefore went to see the war minister on January 23, 1936 and told him: 'If General Watanabe is not removed from office, a group of young officers will assassinate him in the course of an uprising that will be on a larger scale than that of May 1932.' The minister was neither surprised nor dismayed by this announcement; he encouraged Isobe to apply further pressure for Watanabe's dismissal and presented him with a precious bottle of sake, adding: 'But please act prudently.'[46]

On January 28, Isobe was received again by Mazaki and this time told him about the planned rebellion. Mazaki promised to secure the needed financial support but asked not to be informed about the affair in advance.[47] A few days before the outbreak of the rebellion, on

---

39   磯部浅一

40   荒木貞夫，真崎甚三郎

41   古荘幹郎

42   Isobe Asaichi, 'Kōdōki 行動記', in Kōno, p. 32.

43   As stated in General Mazaki's verdict; see *The Japan Advertiser*, September 23, 1937; also Isobe, in Kōno, p. 33.

44   渡辺錠太郎. Ōtani, p. 293.

45   村上啓作. Isobe, in Kōno, p. 38.

46   Isobe, in Kōno, pp. 36–7.

47   Isobe, in Kōno, p. 37; Isobe, *Bungei*, VI. 3, 266.

February 15, the whole group of plotters, headed by Andō and Isobe, was received by Major General Yamashita at his house. At that meeting, the general told his junior guests, many of whom he had known personally from the time he was commander of the Third Infantry Regiment, that Prime Minister Okada should be cut down first, and then, when martial law was proclaimed, additional traitors could be destroyed.[48]

This support from high echelons of the army delighted the rebels, but it was not enough. In order to succeed, they had to be sure of the support, or at least the neutrality, of other sources of power, such as the navy, the business world, the Diet and the Court, none of which they neglected in their meticulous planning.

The group in the navy on whose support the rebels counted most was the Fleet faction (Kantaiha),[49] which sharply opposed the navy leadership on account of the latter's endorsement of the London Naval Treaty. But this faction, headed by Admiral Yamamoto Eisuke and Reserve Admiral Katō Kanji,[50] was mostly out of power and could exercise only a moral influence. Also, among the members of this faction were Admiral Yamamoto Isoroku, the head of the navy's Aviation Command, and Rear Admiral Mazaki Katsuji, General Mazaki's younger brother.[51]

Another channel for influencing the navy was the retired Admiral Viscount Ogasawara Naganari, a protégé of Tōgō Heihachirō and a former tutor of the emperor, as well as a friend of Nishida Mitsugi,[52] the rebels' civilian collaborator. Admiral Ogasawara also had good relations with the naval chief of staff, Admiral Prince Fushimi.[53]

The considerable support which the rebels were beginning to gain made them attractive to some sections of the business world. As early as 1934, Mitsui had put Kita Ikki on a lavish payroll.[54] In

[48] Isobe, in Kōno, p. 47; Arai Isao 新井勲, *Nihon o shinkansaseta yokkakan* 日本を震撼させた四日間 (Tokyo: Bungei Shunjū Shinsha, 1949), p. 124; Oki, pp. 225–6.

[49] 艦隊派

[50] 山本英輔, 加藤寛治

[51] 山本五十六, 真崎勝次. Ōtani, p. 300; Hata, p. 122; Harada Kumao 原田熊雄, *Saionji kō to seikyoku* 西園寺公と政局 (Tokyo: Iwanami Shoten, 1950–6), v, 110; *Nihon kindaishi jiten*, p. 726.

[52] 西田税

[53] 伏見宮. Ōtani, pp. 77–8; Yukawa Kōhei 湯川康平, 'Ni ni-roku jiken to Saionji kō 二・二六事件と西園寺公', *Bungei shunjū*, xLV. 6 (June 1967), 327. (Yukawa is the later surname of Kiyohara 清原 Kōhei, former second lieutenant of the Third Regiment and a participant in the February 1936 rebellion.)

[54] 三井. As admitted by Kita at his interrogation; Tanaka Sōgorō 田中惣五郎, *Nihon fuasshizumu no genryū* 日本ファ*

July 1935, Mitsui's head, Ikeda Seihin,[55] advised Prince Saionji against the removal of General Mazaki from his post as inspector general of military education.[56] That year Ikeda Seihin paid Kita 30,000 yen ($8,400),[57] part of which found its way to the rebels. Mitsui's interests, as well as Ikeda's life, were thus safeguarded in case the rebellion succeeded. With Mitsui backing the rebels, it might be Mitsubishi's turn to support their opponents. On February 19, 1936, Mitsubishi's head office informed the military police about the secret meeting which the rebels had held the day before and in which the full details of the insurrection had been worked out.[58]

Mitsui was not the only zaibatsu[59] supporting the rebels. Ishihara Kōichirō, the head of the Ishihara Industries and a long-time rightist sympathizer, donated 3,000 yen ($840) to them through Lieutenant Kurihara.[60] Another supporter of the rebels who represented both business and politics was Kuhara Fusanosuke,[61] the head of an industrial concern which included such companies as Nissan and Hitachi, and the leader of the right-wing faction of the Seiyūkai in the House of Representatives. Kuhara gave the rebels 5,000 yen ($1,400) through his friend Kamekawa Tetsuya, who was in contact with them.[62]

In the House of Peers the rebels could count on the support of the president, Prince Konoe Fumimaro,[63] an old friend of General Araki and a sympathizer with the young officers' movement. Rumor even had it that part of the rebels' financial support came from Prince Konoe and people close to him.[64]

The intensive preparations for the rebellion could not escape the notice of the police. At the end of January 1936, both the Tokyo Military Police and the Tokyo Metropolitan Police were informed of

---

*ッシズムの源流 (Tokyo: Hakuyōsha, 1949), p. 335.

55 池田成彬

56 Harada, IV, 293.

57 As admitted by Ikeda at his interrogation; see Matsumoto Seichō 松本清張, *Shōwa shi hakkutsu* 昭和史発掘 (Tokyo: *Bungei shunjū*, 1969), VIII, 255.

58 三菱. Hata, p. 139.

59 三井

60 Fukumoto Kameji 福本亀治, *Hei ni tsugu* 兵に告ぐ (Tokyo: Yamato Shobō, 1954), pp. 208–9. (At the time of the rebellion Fukumoto was chief of the Special Service Section [Tokkōka] of the Tokyo Military Police.)

61 久原房之助

62 Harada, VI, 49–50; Fukumoto, p. 140.

63 近衛文麿

64 Yabe Teiji 矢部貞治, *Konoe Fumimaro* 近衛文麿 (Tokyo: Jiji Tsūshin, 1958), pp. 60–3; Oki, p. 222.

them. When they reported their findings to the headquarters of the Tokyo garrison, they were told not to worry. The Tokyo Military Police, which asked for reinforcements, was told by the Military Police Command that they were not needed. Further suggestions by the Tokyo Military Police of plans to crush a possible insurrection were rejected by the War Ministry.[65]

On the night of February 17, Second Lieutenant Tokiwa Minoru[66] took out his whole company to rehearse the attack on the Metropolitan Police. When the startled police officers saw the soldiers charging their building time after time with fixed bayonets, they protested to the First Division, to which the soldiers belonged. The Division, however, replied that those were necessary maneuvers for the soldiers' combat duties in Manchuria. When similar rehearsals were conducted on the following nights around the prime minister's residence and again around the Metropolitan Police, the police authorities complained to the headquarters of the Tokyo garrison, but were answered again that the night drills of the Imperial Army were none of the business of the Tokyo police.[67]

Was Isobe then indulging in wishful thinking when he was telling his comrades that the rebellion was going to succeed because important people were behind it?[68] Or were the enthusiastic junior officers wrong when, urging one of their comrades to join them, they told him: 'All kinds of people are now involved in it' (*iroiro te mo utte aru*)?[69] There was still another reason for their self-confidence: channels had been found to the Imperial Throne.

Paths to The Throne

The most important lesson that the rebels of February 1936 had learned from previous failures, as well as from the success of the Meiji Restoration, was that only by enlisting the charismatic support of the emperor could a national reform succeed. As Professor Hall

---

[65] Harada, IV, 413; Fukumoto, pp. 102–8; Ōtani Keijirō 大谷敬二郎, *Shōwa kempei shi* 昭和憲兵史 (Tokyo: Misuzu Shobō, 1966), pp. 159–62.

[66] 常盤稔

[67] *Keishichō shi* 警視庁史 (Tokyo: Keishichō Shi Hensan Iinkai 警視庁

史編纂委員会, 1962), *Shōwa zempen* 昭和前編, p. 446; Ōtani, *Shōwa kempei shi*, p. 160; Isobe, in Kōno, p. 47.

[68] Isobe, in Kōno, p. 38.

[69] Yukawa, *Bungei shunjū*, XLV. 6, 327.

has remarked: 'In the history of Japanese factional politics, possession of the emperor was nine-tenths of the game.'[70]

The quickest way of getting hold of the emperor was by seizing his palace and replacing his 'bad' advisers with the 'correct' ones. As it would be unthinkable to storm the palace from the outside, it became necessary to find a way to capture it from within. The clue to that was Lieutenant Nakahashi Motoaki of the Imperial Guards Division, son of an army general and great-grandson of a Saga Rebellion participant. Nakahashi was commander of the Seventh Company of the Third Imperial Guards Regiment and his company was scheduled to begin its duty as the relief unit (*fuen chūtai*)[71] to the Palace Guard on February 26. This duty, which was assigned every week to another company of the Imperial Guards Division, entitled that company to enter the palace grounds in case of emergency to protect the emperor. According to the disclosure of a former rebel officer, the plan was that Nakahashi's unit would enter the palace and open it from within to the rebels, who would then seize the gates and thus control access to the emperor. For this reason the rebellion was scheduled for February 26.[72]

One of the 'correct' advisers who was to supervise the emperor's proper conduct in the first hours of the rebellion was his chief aide-de-camp, General Honjō Shigeru.[73] Honjō was not only a personal friend of Generals Araki (by whom he had been appointed to that post in 1933) and Mazaki since the time the three of them had attended the same (ninth) class of the Military Academy, but he was also the father-in-law of one of the rebellion's plotters, Captain Yamaguchi Ichitarō.[74] Yamaguchi was scheduled to be the officer of the day in the First Regiment on February 26 and it was his role to let the armed rebel units out. Then he was to contact his father-in-law and arrange with him the reception of General Mazaki by

[70] John Whitney Hall, 'A Monarch for Modern Japan', in Robert E. Ward, ed., *Political Development in Modern Japan* (Princeton: Princeton University Press, 1968), p. 44.

[71] 中橋基明, 赴援中隊

[72] Yukawa Kōhei, Imaizumi Yoshimichi 今泉義道, Ikeda Toshihiko 池田俊彦, and Funaki Shigeru 船木繁, 'Kore ga Shōwa ishin na no da これが昭和維新なのだ', *Bungei shunjū*, XLV. 2 (February 1967), 239–45. Yukawa (formerly Kiyohara), Imaizumi, and Ikeda are the only three surviving rebel officers. Funaki was an officer of the government troops that were scheduled to suppress the rebellion; see also Yukawa, *Bungei shunjū*, XLV. 6, 322.

[73] 本庄繁

[74] Honjō Shigeru 本庄繁, *Honjō nikki* 本庄日記 (Tokyo: Hara Shobō, 1967), p. 271.

the emperor and Mazaki's appointment as the prime minister of a restoration cabinet. Other dignitaries, such as Marquis Tokugawa Yoshichika, were then to assist the emperor to reach the same conclusion.[75]

Prince Saionji, who ordinarily advised the emperor on the appointment of new prime ministers, was initially listed by the rebels for assassination as one of the chief villains around the throne.[76] But on February 25, Kamekawa Tetsuya,[77] Kuhara Fusanosuke's liaison officer with the rebels, after having met twice with General Mazaki, brought before the rebel leaders a new plan concerning the genro. He told them that, as his friend, Aizawa's civilian attorney, Dr. Uzawa Sōmei, was on good terms with the prince, he thought it would be better if Saionji was spared, and through Uzawa persuaded them to recommend General Mazaki as the next prime minister after the outbreak of the rebellion. To give his suggestion more appeal, Kamekawa combined it with the first instalment of the money donated by Kuhara to the rebellion. The rebels were convinced and Saionji's name was struck from the assassination list, less than 24 hours before the outbreak of the rebellion.[78]

Another road to the throne, more fascinating than the previous ones, was through a group of imperial princes on whose tacit support, at least, the rebels could count. One of these was Prince Higashikuni, a paternal uncle of Hirohito,[79] who was also a major general in the army and a member of the SupremeWar Council. Prince Higashikuni was known for his links to various rightist groups. Thus, for instance, after the May Incident of 1932, he paid a personal visit to the Aikyōjuku, Tachibana Kōzaburō's[80] notorious school in Mito, at the time when Tachibana was already under arrest for his part in the affair. This visit prompted the governor of Ibaraki Prefecture to resign in protest.[81] A year later, Higashikuni was mentioned in connection with the Shimpeitai plot, which was led by his friend

[75] Arai, p. 135; Yukawa *et al.*, *Bungei shunjū*, XLV. 2, 245; Ōtani, *Ni ni-roku jiken no nazo*, pp. 77–8; Harada, v, 111.

[76] Isobe, in Kōno, pp. 45–6; *The Japan Advertiser*, July 8, 1936.

[77] 亀川哲也

[78] Fukumoto, pp. 117, 120; Yukawa, *Bungei shunjū*, XLV. 6, 325–6; *The Japan Advertiser*, August 7, 1936; Hata, p. 292.

The official version was that the attack had been called off because of the refusal of Lieutenant Itagaki Tetsu 板垣徹 to participate in it. See *The Japan Advertiser*, July 8, 1936.

[79] He had married Princess Toshiko, Emperor Meiji's ninth daughter.

[80] 愛郷塾, 橘孝三郎

[81] Harada, II, 348.

Yasuda Tatsunosuke.[82] When Aizawa came to Tokyo in the summer of 1935 to kill Nagata, he met first with Prince Higashikuni, who happened to be his former commander in the Twenty-ninth Regiment.[83]

Another prince on whose support the rebels could count was Lieutenant General Asaka, also a paternal uncle of Hirohito[84] and a member of the Supreme War Council. In 1933, the prince made the unprecedented gesture of attending the court-martial of the army cadets who had taken part in the May 1932 Incident.[85] In 1934 he was appointed commander of the Imperial Guards Division and, as such, he met with Aizawa before the murder of Nagata and was even asked by him to be introduced to General Ugaki.[86]

The rebels' strongest supporter in the imperial court was, however, Prince Chichibu, Emperor Hirohito's younger brother. Chichibu was a friend of Nishida Mitsugi from the time they were classmates (thirty-fourth class) in the Military Academy.[87] In 1927 when Nishida organized the clandestine Tenkentō group of young officers, which included such future rebels as Muranaka Kōji and Shibukawa Zensuke, Prince Chichibu gave it his tacit support.[88] When the prince was admitted to the War College in 1928, his education there was personally supervised by the college's head, General Araki.[89]

In 1931, Prince Chichibu was assigned as a company commander to the Third Infantry Regiment in Tokyo, where he soon became a close friend of Andō Teruzo, Nonaka Shirō, and Sakai Naoshi, all of them future leaders of the February 1936 rebellion.[90] The prince's cordial relations with the radical young officers were a well-known fact[91] and even the Soviet Japan-watchers, writing at that time under

[82] Harada, III, 150.

[83] Harada, IV, 320; see also Higashikuni Naruhiko 東久邇稔彦, 'Yancha kōzoku no sensō to heiwa やんちゃ皇族 の戦争と平和', *Bungei shunjū*, XLVI.1 (January 1968), 161. Higashikuni Naruhiko is, of course, the former Prince Higashikuni, and the above article is an interview with him.

[84] He had married Princess Nobuko, Emperor Meiji's eighth daughter.

[85] *The Japan Advertiser*, July 28, 1933.

[86] Harada, IV, 355–6.

[87] Suematsu Tahei 末松太平, *Wata-*

kushi no Shōwa shi 私の昭和史 (Tokyo: Misuzu Shobō, 1963), p. 21. Suematsu was a friend of the Tokyo rebels, but he was stationed in Aomori at the time of the rebellion.

[88] *Gendaishi shiryō*, IV, 37, 39; Suematsu, p. 25.

[89] Kikkawa Manabu 橘川学, *Arashi to tatakau tesshō Araki* 嵐と闘う哲将荒木 (Tokyo: Araki Sadao Shōgun Denki Hensan Kankōkai, 1955), p. 108.

[90] Arai, pp. 242–4.

[91] Higashikuni, *Bungei shunjū*, XLVI. 1, 170; Suematsu, p. 230.

the pseudonyms Tanin and Yohan, noticed it.[92] In the May 1932 Incident, Prince Chichibu's relations with the young officers became so flagrant that they invited a later rebuke from the emperor himself.[93] In September 1932 Prince Konoe recommended Prince Chichibu for the post of lord keeper of the privy seal, a position which would have given him great power over the emperor. But this was vetoed by Prince Saionji.[94] Instead the prince was assigned to the General Staff. The young officers of the Third Regiment continued to visit Chichibu at his home, and at one of these visits he is said to have promised them to come to their support in case of an insurrection.[95] In 1934 Prince Chichibu's name was involved in the Shimpeitai Affair of the previous year.[96] In August 1935, when General Mazaki was transferred from his post as inspector general of military education, Major Chichibu was transferred from Tokyo to faraway Hirosaki.

Prince Chichibu was not only an imperial prince. Until Prince Akihito's birth in December 1933, he was also the apparent heir to the throne and would have become emperor had Hirohito died or abdicated for reasons of health, as did his father. It is significant that, in the early 1930s, critical remarks began to be made against the emperor by such army men as General Mazaki, court princes such as Higashikuni and other dignitaries such as Prince Konoe.[97]

The rebels themselves, in spite of their reverence for the imperial institution, would have shed few tears if Hirohito had abdicated in favor of his brother or his minor son with his brother as regent. As Isobe put it later in his prison diary: 'Your majesty, how badly you conduct the affairs of the state! . . . If you pursue this course any longer, you will certainly arouse the wrath of the gods. You are now the emperor, but if you stray from the way of the gods, you shall forfeit your throne.'[98]

---

[92] O. Tanin and E. Yohan, *Militarism and Fascism in Japan* (New York: International Publishers, 1934), p. 182.

[93] Kido Kōichi 木戸幸一, *Kido Kōichi nikki* 木戸幸一日記 (Tokyo: Tōkyō Daigaku Shuppankai, 1966), I, 468.

[94] Harada, II, 343.

[95] Arai, pp. 244–5; Hara Keigo 原

敬吾, 'Ni ni-roku jiken ni tsuite hitotsu no uwasa 二・二六事件について一つの噂', *Kokoro*, May 1966, p. 64.

[96] Harada, IV, 155.

[97] Harada, II, 47, 66, 338–9; Higashikuni, *Bungei shunjū*, XLVI.1, 162.

[98] Isobe Asaichi, 'Gokuchū nikki', in Hashikawa, pp. 174–5.

Two Days of Success

The units which went into action in the early morning of February 26 encountered little or no resistance and, within a couple of hours, achieved most of their goals. The lord keeper of the privy seal, Admiral Saitō Makoto, the inspector general of military education, General Watanabe Jōtarō, and Finance Minister Takahashi Kore-kiyo lay dead in their bedrooms.[99] Prime Minister Okada Keisuke was pronounced dead and it mattered little for the moment that he was actually hiding in his maid's closet.[100] Chief Chamberlain Admiral Suzuki Kantarō was severely wounded and the fate of former lord keeper of the privy seal Makino Nobuaki, whose inn had been burned down, was unclear.[101]

The other military units in Tokyo, which outnumbered the fourteen hundred rebel troops, did not stir, and both the Military Police and the Tokyo Metropolitan Police watched passively as the rebels occupied the War Ministry, the General Staff, police headquarters, and other government buildings in the center of the capital. Lieutenant Nakahashi succeeded in entering the Imperial Palace and seized the southern and western gates, which bordered on the area occupied by the rebels. The gates to the north and the east, however, remained under the control of the Palace Guard.[102]

Neither General Hori, the commander of the First Division, from which the bulk of the rebels had come, nor the regimental commanders, Colonels Kofuji Megumu and Shibuya Masao,[103] made any attempt that morning to order their troops back to the barracks. Later in the day, the troops were ordered to supply the rebels with food.[104] The military policemen stationed in the occupied area collaborated by serving as guards to the buildings seized by the rebels.[105]

[99] 斎藤実, 渡辺錠太郎, 高橋是清

[100] His brother-in-law, Colonel Matsuo Denzō 松尾伝蔵, was mistaken for him and killed. *Ni ni-roku jiken hanketsu gempon to kankei shiryō* 二・二六事件判決原本［付］関係資料 (Tokyo: Tōchōsha, 1964), p. 289. There is also a possibility that Lieutenant Nibu Seichū, Okada's relative and one of the rebel officers, arranged the saving of the prime minister's life, as hinted by Fukumoto, p. 139.

[101] 牧野伸顕

[102] As revealed by Imaizumi, who had taken part in the attack on the palace. Yukawa *et al.*, *Bungei shunjū*, XLV. 2, 245.

[103] 小藤恵, 渋谷正雄

[104] Tanaka, p. 364; Kinoshita Hanji 木下半治, *Nihon fuashizumu shi* 日本ファシズム史 (Tokyo: Iwasaki Shoten, 1949–51), II, 430.

[105] Ōtani, *Shōwa kempei shi*, p. 164.

When the news reached the chiefs of the War Ministry, many of them expressed delight.[106] The Kōdō generals of the Supreme War Council went immediately into action: General Araki contacted the chief of the Metropolitan Police and asked him not to intervene;[107] General Mazaki dispatched Dr. Uzawa to Okitsu to enlist the support of Prince Saionji. Uzawa returned later without having found the prince.[108]

In the meantime, at his home, War Minister Kawashima received the rebel leaders, who read to him their manifesto and submitted a list of demands—for example, that their true motives be conveyed to the emperor, that high-ranking Kōdō officers be summoned for consultations and that some Tōsei officers be dismissed from office.[109] Kawashima seemed inclined to consent to these demands: he ordered that the rebels' manifesto be distributed among all army units[110] and that the requested Kōdō generals be summoned. Major General Yamashita, who came first, greeted the rebel leaders cordially; retired General Saitō Ryū, who came next, addressed them as the 'righteous army' (*gigun*);[111] and General Mazaki, who arrived last, congratulated them, saying: 'At last you have done it. I understand you well.'[112] At the meeting with those generals it was decided to send General Kawashima to the emperor to convey the rebels' motives.

The enraged emperor was probably surprised to discover that morning that his top military advisers, the chief aide-de-camp, General Honjō, and War Minister Kawashima, were both sympathetic to the rebels. At first, General Honjō told the emperor what had happened, but when he was ordered to see to it that the 'rioters' (*bōto*) were immediately suppressed, the general asked the emperor not to apply such harsh terms to his loyal troops.[113] Then came General Kawashima, fresh from his meeting with the Kōdō generals, to read to his majesty the rebels' manifesto.[114] The emperor repeated his order to crush the 'rioters', but no one seemed to heed him. The War Ministry, instead of moving to quell the insurrection, was busy

---

106 Fukumoto, p. 141.

107 Kikkawa, pp. 398–9.

108 *Gendaishi shiryō*, IV, 176; Ōtani, *Ni ni-roku jiken no nazo*, pp. 298–9.

109 Hata, p. 142.

110 Isobe, in Kōno, p. 58; Kinoshita, II, 383.

111 斎藤瀏

112 Isobe, in Kōno, pp. 58–60; Ōtani, *Shōwa kempei shi*, pp. 167–8; Hata, p. 294.

113 Harada, V, 6.

114 Honjō, p. 272; Harada, V, 7.

preparing the draft of a 'proclamation of restoration' (*ishin taishō*)[115] to be issued by the emperor. The draft, formulated by the Military Affairs Section, headed by the Kōdō Colonel Murakami Keisaku, followed, in general terms, the rebels' manifesto and was submitted on that day to the war minister.[116] General Araki, in the meantime, prepared a file of previous imperial proclamations and brought it to the palace.[117]

The Supreme War Council, which met that afternoon at the Imperial Palace, was dominated by the Kōdō generals Araki and Mazaki, their sympathizers, Generals Abe Nobuyuki and Nishi Giichi, and Princes Higashikuni and Asaka.[118] After some deliberations the council adopted a declaration, to be issued by the war minister, in support of the rebels' cause. The declaration recognized the rebels' sincere motives which, it stated, had been reported to the emperor. It then pledged the support of all the council members for the implementation of the rebels' lofty ideals. The declaration finished by saying that the emperor's decision was being awaited.[119]

Major General Yamashita hurried with the declaration's draft to the rebel leaders, who were waiting at the war minister's residence, and read it to them three times.[120] A couple of hours later, the Tokyo Garrison Command issued a printed form of the declaration, which was even more in support of the rebels. Instead of the adopted version which had stated that the rebels' 'true motives' (*shin'i*) had been recognized, the printed one said that the rebels' 'actions' (*kōdō*) were recognized.[121] This meant that the highest military authorities, including two imperial princes, had convened at the palace and approved the rebellion, including the assassinations and the occupation. In other words, the insurgents became loyal troops acting for lofty purposes.[122]

Following the war minister's declaration, the Tokyo garrison

---

115 維新大詔

116 Kōno, pp. 114–15; Ōtani, *Ni ni-roku jiken no nazo*, pp. 193–4.

117 Ōtani, *Ni ni-roku jiken no nazo*, p. 180.

118 阿部信行, 西義一, 東久邇 (宮), 朝香 (宮)

119 Isobe, *Bungei*, VI. 3, 252; Kōno, pp. 411–13; *Ni ni-roku jiken hanketsu gempon to kankei shiryō*, p. 273. Yamashita later argued that the declaration

had been issued as a device to lure the rebels to withdraw, but this fails to explain the fact that no such demand had been mentioned in the declaration.

120 Isobe, *Bungei*, VI. 3, 252; Ōtani, *Ni ni-roku jiken no nazo*, p. 204.

121 Isobe, *Bungei*, VI.3, 253; Kōno, p. 412.

122 Ōtani, *Ni ni-roku jiken no nazo*, pp. 205–6.

proclaimed a state of 'war-time defense' (*senji keibi*)[123] in the area under the rebels' occupation and assigned to the rebels, who were now officially called 'action units' (*kōdō butai*),[124] the task of patrolling that area. Colonel Kofuji, the pro-Kōdō commander of the First Regiment, was appointed as their commander.[125] It seemed now that the army had endorsed the rebellion and was going to carry out its declared purpose of a Shōwa restoration. At least that was how the rebel officers, their soldiers, and many others in the army and the military police felt.[126]

The first official announcement to the public about what had happened was issued by the War Ministry at 8:15 that evening. It described briefly the assassinations, without telling about Takahashi's death, and gave a lengthy summary of the rebels' manifesto.[127] There was no mention of the occupation and no censure of the whole affair. That night the cabinet decided, at the request of the army and despite the opposition of the navy, to proclaim martial law in Tokyo.[128]

The Martial Law Proclamation, signed by the emperor on the morning of February 27, did not mention the rebellion at all. It gave as cause for the martial law the sudden danger of an outburst by 'Communist elements', which was to be suppressed.[129] According to the proclamation, the Tokyo garrison became the Martial Law Headquarters. The 'action units' became the patrolling arm of the martial law authorities in the center of Tokyo. The fact that the Martial Law Proclamation was signed by the emperor could mean, as it meant to Isobe, that the rebellion had been approved by his majesty.[130] Soon afterwards, the army stopped the bringing in of reinforcements to the capital.[131] The rebels reacted by reducing their occupation to the Miyakezaka area, south of the Imperial Palace.[132]

---

123 戦時警備

124 行動部隊

125 *Ni ni-roku jiken hanketsu gempon to kankei shiryō*, p. 273.

126 Isobe, *Bungei*, VI.3, 254; Ōtani, *Ni ni-roku jiken no nazo*, pp. 200–1, 214; Yukawa, *Bungei shunjū*, XLV. 6, 322; Kuratomo Otokira, 'Ichiheishi no Ni ni-roku jiken' 一兵士の二・二六事件, *Bungei shunjū*, XLVI.1 (January 1968), 325. Kuratomo was a soldier in the rebel forces.

127 *The Japan Advertiser*, February

27, 1936.

128 Kido, I, 465–6; Ōtani, *Ni ni-roku jiken no nazo*, p. 16.

129 *Tōkyō nichinichi shimbun* 東京日日新聞, February 28, 1936, evening edition; *The Japan Advertiser*, February 28, 1936.

130 Isobe, *Bungei*, VI.3, 255; see also Kōda's similar reaction, in Kōno, p. 222.

131 Harada, VI, 31.

132 *Gendaishi shiryō*, IV, 176; Isobe, in Kōno, p. 71; *The Japan Advertiser*, July 8, 1936.

The apparent success of the rebellion brought about a favorable reaction in certain civilian circles, especially among the rightists and the lower classes. On the evening of February 26, groups of citizens began flocking to the rebel positions, congratulating them for their deeds and addressing them as 'the revolutionary army' (*kakumei gun*) or 'the light of the poor'.[133] On the next day the expressions of popular support increased: rightist groups, Nichiren believers, reservists and young people came to the rebels' headquarters, blowing trumpets, cheering, and asking the rebel officers to make speeches.[134] Even the civilian police began to collaborate by supplying the rebels with needed information.[135] It is no wonder that on February 28 the rebel officers and soldiers were celebrating their victory by 'drinking and singing without their shoes on'.[136]

In the afternoon of that day, Prince Chichibu came to Tokyo from his assignment post in Hirosaki, defying a special request of the Imperial Household Ministry that he not do so.[137] Arriving at the palace, Chichibu conferred with Generals Honjō and Kawashima and then went to see his elder brother. Soon afterwards the emperor agreed to receive General Mazaki in audience.[138]

Everything seemed ready for the restoration: the chief villains were slain or had disappeared, the unprecedented military insurrection had been explicitly approved by the army and implicitly recognized by the emperor, and now the emperor's brother and possible heir to his throne had apparently demonstrated his sympathy with the rebels. The only thing still lacking was the emperor's explicit consent.

The Failure

The emperor refused to sanction any restoration and his constant and firm opposition to the rebellion became one, although not the only, cause for its failure. When he received General Mazaki on the evening of February 27, Hirohito did not appoint him head of a new

[133] Kuratomo, *Bungei shunjū*, XLVI.1, 325; Hayashi Hiroichi, *Kakumei narazu* 革命ならず (Tokyo: Mainichi Shimbunsha, 1959), p. 45.

[134] Isobe, in Kōno, p. 71.

[135] Yukawa, *Bungei shunjū*, XLV.6, 322.

[136] Harada, v, 31.

[137] Kiya Ikusaburō 木舍幾三郎, *Konoe kō hibun* 近衛公秘聞 (Tokyo: Takanoyama Shuppansha, 1950), pp. 20–1.

[138] *The Tokyo Nichi Nichi* and *The Osaka Mainichi*, February 29, 1936; Harada, v, 5; Tanaka, p. 365.

cabinet, but rather admonished him for not having suppressed the rebellion.[139]

The longer the emperor resisted the pressure to appoint a prime minister favorable to the rebels, the easier it became for the Tōsei-dominated General Staff to muster the strength necessary to crush the rebellion. Without the full support of the emperor, the rebels could not force a Shōwa restoration on the reluctant government. On the other hand, without the full backing of the government they could not force their demands on the emperor or make him abdicate. The lack of either full political power or an outright imperial endorsement made the rebels' position precarious and enabled their opponents to recover from an initial defeat.

The strongest of these opponents proved at first to be not the General Staff, which was paralyzed by the attitude of the war minister and the Supreme War Council, but the navy, which was traditionally opposed to any increase in the army's political influence. The navy was also upset by the fact that three of the five attacked and presumably murdered leaders, Okada, Saitō and Suzuki, were admirals. Although the chief of the naval staff, Prince Fushimi, maintained close relations with both Mazaki and Katō Kanji during the rebellion and seems to have favored the rebels' cause,[140] the majority of the navy command was strongly opposed to the rebellion. On February 26, at 10:00 a.m., Admiral Yonai Mitsumasa,[141] the commander of the Yokosuka Naval Station near Tokyo, ordered the First Torpedo Squadron to land marines and tanks in Shibaura Ward to provide protection for the Navy Ministry, which bordered on the area occupied by the rebels. Soon afterwards the navy ordered the combined fleet to hurry home from its maneuvers at sea and enter Tokyo and Osaka bays.[142] On the afternoon of February 27, forty ships of the First Fleet entered Tokyo Bay and lined up along the city's coast line, with their guns aimed at the capital. In case the situation worsened, the emergency plan of the navy was to rescue the emperor from the rebels' hands, take him to a battleship, and then to

139 Harada, v, 5.

140 Takahashi Masae 高橋正衛, *Ni ni-roku jiken* 二・二六事件 (Tokyo: Chūō Kōronsha, 1965), pp. 61, 160; see also Andō's words of praise for Admiral Fushimi in his prison testament; Kōno, p. 180.

141 米内光政

142 Takamiya Tahei 高宮太平, *Yonai Mitsumasa* 米内光政 (Tokyo: Jiji Tsū-shinsha, 1958), p. 43; *The Japan Advertiser*, February 27, 1936; Takahashi, p. 85.

bombard the city. For that purpose, additional troops were landed in Tokyo and rushed to strategic points.[143]

On the evening of February 26, the navy protested to the army over the war minister's distorted declaration, and the Tokyo Garrison was ordered to issue a corrected version of it, limiting the recognition again to the rebels' motives.[144] On February 27 the navy rejected the so-called Imperial Hotel proposal, worked out the night before by Ishihara Kanji of the General Staff and Muranaka Kōji of the rebels, with Hashimoto Kingorō as mediator, under which Admiral Yamamoto Eisuke, of the Kantai naval faction, would be appointed as prime minister.[145] On the same day Admiral Shimada Shigetarō, the vice chief of the naval staff, told General Sugiyama Gen, the vice chief of the army's general staff, that the navy was ready to assist in the suppression of the rebellion.[146] The rebels' efforts to secure the navy's neutrality, through their connections with Admirals Katō Kanji and Ogasawara Naganari, had failed.[147]

Toward the end of that day, February 27, it became evident that instead of a clear-cut victory for the rebels, the situation had developed into a stalemate in which the rebels held the center of Tokyo and enjoyed the support of the Tokyo garrison, the War Ministry, and the Supreme War Council, while the navy, the General Staff and the emperor opposed them, and the rest of Japan was watching passively. They were like two enormous *sumō* wrestlers, each trying desperately to knock the other out of the ring.

At first, it seemed as if the rebels would attempt to make the decisive move. Having failed to achieve a restoration cabinet and sensing the growing opposition, they began to prepare, on the night of February 27, for a new attack on the strongholds of their opponents. It was now the turn of the other *sumōtori* to respond and so, in the early hours of February 28, the General Staff succeeded in obtaining an imperial command, ordering the Martial Law Headquarters to

---

[143] Hata, p. 122; Takahashi, pp. 85–6; Takamiya, *Yonai*, p. 43.

[144] Ōtani, *Ni ni-roku jiken no nazo* p. 209; and 'Ni ni-roku jiken no nazo o toku 二・二六事件の謎を解く', *Kaizō*, 改造, XXXII.2 (February 1951), 160. The latter is a symposium participated in by men who had been involved in the rebellion, including former prime minister

Okada and Yasui Tōji 安井藤次, former chief of staff of the Tokyo Garrison.

[145] *Gendaishi shiryō*, IV, 176; Kido, I, 467; Takahashi, pp. 90–2.

[146] Hata, p. 297; 'Ni ni-roku jiken no nazo o toku', *Kaizō*, XXXII.2, 159.

[147] Harada, V, 43; Hata, p. 294; *Gendaishi shiryō*, IV, 177.

expel the 'occupying units' *(senryō butai)* immediately from their positions.[148] This imperial command was unusual because it contradicted former orders which recognized the rebels as official troops. Nevertheless, it made further resistance by the rebels appear as defiance of the emperor's will and prevented the Tokyo garrison from siding openly with the rebels.

Soon after receiving the imperial command, the head of the Martial Law Headquarters, General Kashii,[149] requested the General Staff to allow him to postpone its implementation so that he could, in the meantime, meet with the emperor and advise him to proclaim a Shōwa restoration. The vice chief of staff, General Sugiyama, rejected the proposal and demanded that General Kashii carry out the order. When General Araki tried to intervene in favor of the rebels, he was asked to leave the conference room by Colonel Ishihara Kanji.[150]

General Kashii had to comply and relay the imperial order to the two divisions under his command but, whereas the Imperial Guards Division began immediately to prepare for a military confrontation with the rebels, the First Division was more reluctant to do so. The divisional commander, General Hori, assured the rebels that he would prevent the Imperial Guards Division from reassuming its command over Lieutenant Nakahashi and his unit, which had been incorporated into the 'action units'.[151] Colonel Kofuji, commander of both the First Regiment and the 'action units', did not convey the imperial command to his rebel troops.[152] Later in the day, however, General Kashii was summoned by the emperor and reprimanded for not having carried out the imperial command.[153] This, together with the constant pressure of the General Staff, forced him to begin serious preparations for suppressing the rebellion.

The rebels had known about the content of the imperial command,[154] but they could claim, as they eventually did, that it was never formally presented to them and that they obeyed their last

---

[148] *Ni ni-roku jiken hanketsu gempon to kankei shiryō*, p. 279.

[149] 香椎

[150] Ōtani, *Ni ni-roku jiken no nazo*, pp. 176–7, 215–16; Takahashi, pp. 105–7.

[151] Ōtani, *Ni ni-roku jiken no nazo*, pp. 226–8; *Gendaishi shiryō*, IV, 178;

Isobe, in Kōno, p. 79.

[152] *The Japan Advertiser*, July 8, 1936.

[153] Harada, V, 7.

[154] Captain Yamaguchi, Honjō's son-in-law, kept them regularly informed about it. Ōtani, *Ni ni-roku jiken no nazo*, pp. 192, 227; Takahashi, p. 102.

orders: to patrol Kōjimachi Ward.[155] They could also claim, as some of them later did, that the imperial command was a forged document, written by the traitors of the General Staff, which did not bind them.[156] It was even said that Prince Chichibu was of the same opinion.[157] Ultimately, they could argue, as Isobe later did, that the Shōwa restoration was more important than the personal opinions of Hirohito and that great heroes of the past, like Saigō Takamori, had never been afraid to oppose a misguided emperor.[158] Kita Ikki, for instance, advised the rebels to disregard the imperial command, which was, in his words, a device of the General Staff to frighten them.[159]

After long deliberations, the rebels decided to ask for a personal 'imperial messenger' *(chokushi)*[160] to convey the emperor's real wishes to them. If the emperor disapproved of their deeds, they would then commit *seppuku*.[161] The request was passed through the Tokyo garrison and the War Ministry to the emperor's chief aide-de-camp, General Honjō, who asked the emperor to grant it. The emperor, however, rejected the appeal, claiming that the rebels had to commit suicide on their own.[162]

The negative reply of the emperor, far from disheartening the rebels, made them finally decide to oppose by force any government troops who might try to suppress them.[163] They got information to the effect that many soldiers and officers of the opposing camp would refuse to shoot at them if ordered to do so,[164] and, in case fighting did erupt, the resolute rebels had a chance to beat the more apathetic government troops.[165] One of the company commanders

[155] 'Ni ni-roku jiken no nazo o toku', *Kaizō*, XXXII.2, 160.

[156] Isobe, in Hashikawa, pp. 178–9; Yukawa, *Bungei shunjū*, XLV.6, 323.

[157] Kinoshita, II, 385.

[158] Isobe, in Hashikawa, pp. 179–80; Ōtani, *Ni ni-roku jiken no nazo*, p. 235.

[159] *Gendaishi shiryō*, IV, 178; also Harada, VI, 32.

[160] 勅使

[161] Isobe, in Kōno, p. 78; Isobe, *Bungei*, VI.3, 251.

[162] Honjō, pp. 277–8.

[163] Isobe, in Kōno, p. 80; Isobe, *Bungei*, VI.3, 251; *The Japan Advertiser*, July 8, 1936.

[164] Koga Fumitake 古賀文武, the civilian who assisted the rebels, was told by many soldiers of the government side that they would not shoot at the rebels. This is revealed by Koga himself in 'Ni ni-roku jiken no nazo o toku', *Kaizō*, XXXII.2, 159–60. Captain Yamashita of the Imperial Guards Division told Isobe the same thing; Isobe, in Kōno, pp. 81, 83.

[165] This was also the opinion of Funaki Shigeru, at that time a second lieutenant in the government camp, as stated by him in Yukawa *et al.*, *Bungei shunjū*, XLV.2, 245.

assigned to suppress the rebels, Lieutenant Arai Isao[166] from the First Regiment of the Imperial Guards Division, deserted the government camp with his men and, for a while, seized the Yasukuni Shrine.[167] The rebel officers still had some hope when they encouraged their soldiers for the coming battle and heard them respond with loud cries of 'banzai'.[168]

But those who were best qualified to judge the trend of events in the army, like the Kōdō generals who had supported the rebels, knew that the moment had arrived for them to back out of the rebellion before they were branded as traitors. During the noon hour on February 28, Generals Yamashita and Hori appeared before the rebels and advised them to surrender.[169] At 4:45 p.m. General Honjō approached the emperor, with tears in his eyes, trying to explain that the army had never defied the emperor's wishes. General Araki was then summoned to the palace and he, too, agreed that the only way to carry out the imperial command was to suppress the rebels by force.[170] Generals Mazaki and Abe gave their consent as supreme war councillors to the use of the Imperial Guards Division for suppressing the insurrection.[171] War Minister Kawashima sent a special letter to the commander of the First Division, General Hori, explaining that, although the rebels' motives were lofty, they had violated military discipline and therefore had to be crushed.[172] Even Prince Chichibu was anxious to put an honorable end to the whole affair and he advised the rebels to commit suicide.[173]

The rebellion was, however, not suppressed by the use of force but rather by the threat of its use, combined with psychological warfare, aimed at the soldiers under the rebels' command. On the morning of February 29, after the civilian population of Kōjimachi Ward was evacuated and the emperor, with Prince Chichibu, had been taken to an 'observation post',[174] tanks carrying posters began entering the rebels' area. The posters called on the soldiers to defy

166 新井勲

167 Arai, pp. 204–5; Fukumoto, p. 128; Yukawa *et al.*, *Bungei shunjū*, XLV.2, 245.

168 Isobe, in Kōno, pp. 80–2.

169 *Gendaishi shiryō*, IV, 178; Isobe, *Bungei*, VI.3, 251; *The Japan Advertiser*, July 8, 1936.

170 Honjō, pp. 278–9.

171 Harada, V, 7.

172 *Ni ni-roku jiken hanketsu gempon to kankei shiryō*, p. 279.

173 Yukawa, *Bungei shunjū*, XLV.6, 323.

174 *Ni ni-roku jiken hanketsu gempon to kankei shiryō*, p. 321; Takahashi, p. 110; Hara, *Kokoro*, May 1966, pp. 67–8.

the orders of their rebel commanders and return to their barracks. Similar appeals were repeatedly broadcast by radio, distributed through leaflets, and hung from an advertisement balloon.[175]

The first to desert were the men under Lieutenant Nakahashi of the Imperial Guards Division, who had probably felt themselves, from the beginning, to be outsiders in an operation carried out mainly by the First Division. Others soon followed, with the consent of the rebel officers who saw no reason to endanger further the lives of their soldiers. Andō's unit was the last one to leave and did so only on his command.[176]

When the defeated rebel officers gathered at the war minister's residence, Major General Yamashita came to see them and asked if they would commit suicide. At first they said they would do so and were then supplied with white sheets. Then Isobe convinced his comrades that if they had to kill themselves, then all the generals who had supported them, starting with the war minister, should do the same.[177] That could also mean that as long as those influential people were alive and free, there was still hope that things might change for the better. The sheets therefore remained white, except for that of Captain Nonaka, the senior company commander among the rebels, who shot himself.[178] Captain Kōno, who had been wounded in the attack on Makino, committed suicide five days later in the hospital.

That evening, War Minister Kawashima issued a statement condemning the rebellion and describing his efforts in putting it down.[179] Other dignitaries, like Prince Fushimi and General Kashii, were received in audience by the emperor and apologized for the outrageous disturbance.[180] It was left to old General Ugaki Kazushige, who cannot be suspected of sympathizing with the rebels, to remark in his diary that it was strange how those who had set the fire in Tokyo were claiming credit for putting it out.[181]

---

[175] *Tōkyō nichinichi shimbun*, March 1, 1936, evening edition; *The Japan Advertiser*, March 1, 1936.

[176] Isobe, in Kōno, pp. 84–8; Yukawa et al., *Bungei shunjū*, XLV.2, 237; Yukawa, *Bungei shunjū*, XLV.6, 323–4; Honjō, p. 280; Fukumoto, p. 125.

[177] Isobe, in Kōno, pp. 90–1; Isobe, *Bungei*, VI.3, 245; 'Ni ni-roku jiken no nazo o toku', *Kaizō*, XXXII.2, 162; Fukumoto, pp. 172–3.

[178] Isobe, in Kōno, p. 90; Fukumoto, pp. 178–9. For a suggestion that Nonaka was murdered, see 'Ni ni-roku jiken no nazo o toku', *Kaizō*, XXXII.2, 162.

[179] *The Japan Advertiser*, March 1, 1936.

[180] Honjō, p. 280.

[181] Ugaki Kazushige 宇垣一成, *Ugaki nikki* 宇垣日記 (Tokyo: Asahi Shimbunsha, 1954), pp. 217–18.

The end of the story is well known: the Kōdō generals and colonels were temporarily purged from the posts they were holding, but most of them returned to prominence in the next year under the Konoe cabinet. The only general to be put on trial, Mazaki, was acquitted when Konoe became prime minister. The troops who had participated in the rebellion were, with some few exceptions, pardoned and transferred as scheduled to Manchuria. Only the rebel officers, together with their civilian collaborators, paid the full price and were executed, carrying with them to their graves some of the most fascinating political secrets of prewar Japan.

Conclusion

The extensive political connections of the February 1936 rebels indicate that the Affair was of a much more serious character than is usually assumed. It was serious not because extremist junior officers imposed their views on a spineless establishment, but because powerful elements of the establishment had decided to extend their support to a group of fanatic idealists in the lower echelons of the military.

The February 1936 rebellion was not a mere mutiny, although it was later so described by those whose interest was in depicting it as such. The First Division, which provided the great majority of the rebel officers and troops, sympathized with the rebels at all levels of command, including the divisional commander. The Tokyo garrison, which commanded the First and the Imperial Guards Divisions, supported the rebels and so did the war minister and the Supreme War Council. If it was an insurrection, then it was the insurrection of a whole segment of the Japanese military, from top to bottom, against another segment wielding power through the General Staff. The interpretation that the behavior of the authorities was motivated by caution rather than support may apply to the War Ministry and General Staff as a whole, but cannot apply to the influential Kōdō elements in the military establishment which had supported the rebels from the start.

The two rival groups in the army are generally referred to as the Kōdō and Tōsei factions, although, as Professor Crowley has pointed out, the real picture was much more complicated.[182] It is not the

[182] James B. Crowley, 'Japanese Army Factionalism in the Early 1930's', *Journal of Asian Studies*, xxi.3 (May 1962), 309–26.

D

purpose of this study to dwell on the ideological side of the February 26 Affair, but it can be said, in brief, that those associated with the Kōdō faction were more in favor of an etatist-oriented Shōwa restoration than those referred to as members of the Tōsei faction. This was the reason that the reformist young officers were attracted by, and got support from, the Kōdō faction and explains why they were linked together in the abortive rebellion. It may be true that nobody really knew what a Shōwa restoration meant, but then how many of the protagonists of the Meiji Restoration knew beforehand exactly what *it* meant?

The apparent similarity between the attempt to carry out the Shōwa restoration in February 1936 and the way in which the Meiji Restoration had been brought about 68 years earlier did not escape the rebels and their supporters. In both situations the main actors were junior officers (lower samurai) who were highly dedicated to the national cause and who enjoyed the support of their military establishments. In both cases the rebels were aided by influential elements of the old regime and counted on the ultimate support of a sympathetic court clique. The aim in both cases was to establish a new government, which would carry out sweeping political reforms and enhance the nation's military strength.

It is less certain whether the rebels were also aware of the fundamental dissimilarities between the two situations. The Meiji Restoration was carried out in the name of the emperor against the established authority of the Bakufu, which had ruled in its own name. The Shōwa restoration, on the other hand, had to be carried out against a government which ruled in the name of the emperor and enjoyed his personal support. Furthermore, the circumstances had changed so much between these two sets of events that any similarity between them could be dismissed as meaningless. Nevertheless, the myth was there and its existence was sufficient to inspire the rebels to action and persuade others to support them—to an extent that almost spelled success.

Japan's 'New Bureaucrats'
1932–45

ROBERT M. SPAULDING, JR.

ON a warm afternoon in May 1932, a few days after the murder of Prime Minister Inukai by young naval officers, a crowd of reporters gathered outside the residence of Admiral Viscount Saitō Makoto,[1] newly designated to succeed Inukai. One of Saitō's aides began announcing the names of other members of the new cabinet: prominent men with long experience and the dignity of age, nearly all past sixty and two nearing eighty. Suddenly he read the name of Gotō Fumio[2] as new minister of agriculture. The reporters were startled into skeptical laughter, thinking that while Gotō might become secretary to the cabinet he would surely not be a minister.[3]

Their surprise was understandable. At the age of forty-eight, Gotō was joining a cabinet whose other members had an average age of sixty-three. Nothing in his record made him a very likely choice for a cabinet post. Twenty-four years earlier, Gotō had graduated with distinction from the political science faculty of Tokyo Imperial University and placed first among 106 men who passed the administrative examinations for the higher civil service in 1908. In his subsequent career, however, this early promise was only moderately fulfilled. After fourteen years, he became chief of the Home Ministry's powerful Police Bureau, and later deputy governor of Taiwan. But he did not win promotion to the highest career rank, that of vice minister, and in 1930 he resigned from the civil service and accepted the modest security of a life appointment to the House of Peers.

The reason for Gotō's sudden elevation to the cabinet in 1932 was simply that he was a surrogate for the man Saitō really wanted—

---

[1] 斎藤実
[2] 後藤文夫
[3] Morikawa Musei 森川夢声, 'Kanryō no antō: Naimushō no maki', 官僚の暗闘: 内務省の巻, *Nippon hyōron* 日本評論, XIII.3 (March 1938), 175–6.

Izawa Takio, a leader of the second largest political party and a former career bureaucrat who had been Gotō's patron both in the Home Ministry and in Taiwan.[4] Gotō's connection with Izawa and his incongruous presence in a sexagenarian cabinet are facts of slight importance except for one thing: they encouraged speculation that produced the legend of the *shin kanryō* or 'new bureaucrats'.[5] By the end of the Saitō cabinet in 1934, this term had gained currency among Japanese political commentators, and was well on its way to enshrinement in the vocabulary of modern Japanese history.

The name *shin kanryō* was first applied to a small group of bureaucrats who seemed to constitute a new type, somehow distinguishable from their colleagues and predecessors. It was not a name they chose for themselves, but one given them by contemporary journalists, and originally it was at least faintly pejorative.[6] The first 'new bureaucrats', active during the four years of the Saitō and Okada cabinets (1932–6), were not new in the sense of being either particularly youthful or atypical in training and experience. On the contrary, they were well-established career bureaucrats in their forties, holding ranks comparable to those of army colonels and generals, and very much like other civilian bureaucrats in education and career pattern.

What set them apart was a special combination of characteristics: a pragmatic nationalism emphasizing the economic role of the state, a willingness to collaborate with like-minded men in other ministries and in the military services, and a desire to change the existing order from within by non-revolutionary means. In all these respects, the 'new bureaucrats' were fundamentally different from the *seinen shōkō*[7] or young military officers to whom they are sometimes likened. However, these characteristics were not as evident in 1932 as they were five or ten years later, and special circumstances were necessary to bring them to the attention of political commentators.

4 Izawa Takio Denki Hensan Iinkai, 伊沢多喜男伝記編纂委員会 *Izawa Takio* 伊沢多喜男 (Tokyo: Haneda Shoten, 1951), pp. 209–13; and Harada Kumao 原田熊雄, *Saionji kō to seikyoku* 西園寺公と政局 (Tokyo: Iwanami Shoten, 1950–6), II, 295. Gotō wrote the preface to the Izawa biography and was a member of the committee that compiled it.

5 新官僚

6 Itō Kinjirō 伊藤金次郎, 'Shin-kyū kanryō no shōtai 新旧官僚の正体', *Chūō kōron*, LI.9 (September 1936), 120, 122.

7 青年将校

Gotō Fumio's appointment to the Saitō cabinet was the first link in the circumstantial chain.

This 'cabinet of national unity' included a few members of both political parties but was obviously not a party cabinet. The army's flouting of civilian authority with its seizure of Manchuria and the succession of terrorist plots had at least temporarily destroyed the ability of the parties to govern. Yet the army showed little inclination to assume the administrative responsibilities formerly borne by the parties. The result was a power vacuum into which career bureaucrats soon moved. Two early signs of this were Gotō's appointment in May 1932 and the Saitō cabinet's enactment four months later of significant new limitations on the suspension and dismissal of career bureaucrats.[8]

Ironically, both these events resulted primarily from the initiative of a party leader, Izawa Takio of the Minseitō,[9] who not only planted Gotō in the cabinet but sent to Saitō and Gotō a long memorandum urging that dismissal of career civil servants be made more difficult.[10] The chief beneficiaries of the new ordinances were Home Ministry bureaucrats whose tenure in prefectural governorships had been highly unstable during the years of party government. The seeming paradox in these circumstances disappears when one considers Izawa's long bureaucratic background—twenty years in the Home Ministry before his appointment to the House of Peers. He remained essentially a bureaucrat even after he became a powerful figure in party politics. Moreover, he and Gotō continued to be the leaders and patrons of an influential faction of bureaucrats still on active duty in the Home Ministry, including such men as Karasawa Toshiki, Yoshida Shigeru, and Matsumoto Manabu.[11] This group had important connections with other prominent men through two associations that came to be regarded by the public as seedbeds of 'new bureaucrats'—the Kokuikai[12] and the Breakfast Society.

8 Imperial Ordinances 253 and 254 of September 24, 1932.

9 民政党

10 *Izawa Takio*, pp. 213–14.

11 唐沢俊樹, 吉田茂, 松本学. This Yoshida Shigeru is not to be confused with the diplomat of the same name, who became prime minister after World War II.

12 In translation it is difficult to avoid confusing the names Kokuikai 国維会, Kokuhonsha 国本社, and Kenkokukai 建国会, which have very different connotations in Japanese but are all likely to come out in English as 'National Foundation Society' or something similar. The Kokuikai was named after a passage in the Confucian classic known as the *Kuan-tzu* 管子, which cites four virtues as the supports or foundations (*i*) of the nation*

The Kokuikai was an outgrowth of the Kinkei Gakuin or Golden Pheasant Academy founded in 1926 by the Confucian scholar Yasuoka Masaatsu.[13] In this academy, prominent army officers and civilian bureaucrats met periodically to hear lectures by Yasuoka on the philosophy of Wang Yang-ming and its applicability to contemporary Japan. The political significance of this lay both in the prominence of Academy supporters in the civil and military services, and in the historical associations of Wang Yang-ming philosophy in Japan, where even in the seventeenth century its exponents had been notable for their favorable view of Shinto and the Japanese imperial system, and their concern with economic problems, including the plight of farmers.

In January 1932, Yasuoka and several participants in the Golden Pheasant Academy founded a new group called the Kokuikai. Three members of this society were in the Saitō cabinet of May 1932—Agriculture Minister Gotō, War Minister General Araki Sadao, and Foreign Minister Hirota Kōki.[14] The Okada cabinet of July 1934 made the Kokuikai even more conspicuous. Admiral Okada Keisuke[15] entrusted formation of the cabinet to Gotō Fumio, who became home minister and in effect deputy prime minister. Five other bureaucratic members of the Kokuikai received major appointments: Hirota as foreign minister, Fujii Masanobu as finance minister, Kawada Isao as chief cabinet secretary,[16] Karasawa Toshiki as Police Bureau chief, and Yoshida Shigeru of the Home Ministry as Social Affairs Bureau chief. All these men were classified by political writers as 'new bureaucrats'—largely on the basis of their membership in the Kokuikai. Journalists were not alone in equating the two groups. In a private conversation shortly after formation of the Okada cabinet, Prince Saionji asked, 'What on earth are "new bureau-

---

*(*koku* 国): 'The state has four supports—decorum, righteousness, integrity, and sense of shame.' I am indebted to Dr. Tsunoda Jun 角田順 of the National Diet Library for this explanation, which was given to him in the 1930s by a member of the Kokuikai. No doubt unaware of the Japanese society, Chiang K'ai-shek used the same quotation from the *Kuan-tzu* in defining his New Life Movement in 1934. See Liu Wu-chi, *A Short History of Confucian Philosophy* (Balti-

more: Penguin Books, 1955), pp. 106–7, 189–90; Wm. Theodore de Bary *et al.*, comps., *Sources of Chinese Tradition* (New York: Columbia University Press, 1960), pp. 801–2; and Shimmura Izuru 新村出, ed., *Kōjien* 広辞苑 (Tokyo; Iwanami Shoten, 1955), p. 903, s.v. *shii*.

13 金鶏学院, 安岡正篤
14 荒木貞夫, 広田弘毅
15 岡田啓介
16 藤井真信, 河田烈

crats''?' In reply, Marquis Kido Kōichi thought it sufficient to say simply that they were members of the Kokuikai, 'an organization of intellectuals.'[17] By November 1934, gossip about Kokuikai influence in the government had become so embarrassing that the society disbanded—without, of course, withdrawing its members from office.

The 'new bureaucrats' have also been persistently linked with the mysterious Breakfast Society (Asameshikai).[18] Accounts of its origin and composition are so varied that one cannot be sure they all refer to the same group.[19] From numerous entries in the Kido diary, it is certain that meetings under this name were held about once a week from the end of 1931 to the summer of 1935, for private discussion of current political problems, usually at the Tokyo residence of Baron Harada Kumao,[20] Saionji's chief agent and informant. The total number of participants was large, but there were rarely more than fifteen at any one meeting, and the composition of the group varied according to the subject to be discussed. Those who attended most regularly were politically active titled peers, notably Harada, Kido (who was then chief secretary to the lord privy seal), Prince Konoe Fumimaro, and Count Sakai Tadamasa,[21] a Kokuikai founding member who had earlier provided both financial support and the meeting place (in his Tokyo mansion) for the Golden Pheasant Academy.

Prominent career bureaucrats and army officers were less frequent participants, according to the Kido and Harada diaries. The former were mostly 'new bureaucrats' such as Gotō, Karasawa, Yoshida, and the Foreign Ministry's Tani Masayuki and Shiratori Toshio;[22] Izawa Takio also attended occasionally. Military participants included Major General Nagata Tetsuzan, Colonel Inoue Saburō,

---

17 木戸幸一. Harada, IV, 37–8. The conversation took place at Gotemba 御殿場 on August 9, 1934.

18 朝飯会

19 Different writers name Harada, Inoue Saburō 井上三郎, Izawa, Karasawa, Kido, Konoe Fumimaro 近衛文麿, or Nagata Tetsuzan 永田鉄山 as the organizer or chief sponsor. In his diary, Kido used interchangeably the synonymous names Asameshikai, Chōsankai 朝餐会, and Chōshokukai 朝食会 (which differ only in the second of the three

ideographs). All these names are sufficiently generic to have been used concurrently by different groups; on the other hand, lists of participants and descriptions of purpose overlap so extensively as to suggest that only one society may be involved. In either case, there seems to be no connection with the later (1937–1940) Breakfast Society formed by Konoe's secretaries.

20 原田熊雄

21 酒井忠正

22 谷正之, 白鳥敏夫

and Lieutenant Colonel Suzuki Teiichi.[23] Such zaibatsu officials as Ikeda Seihin[24] came to a few meetings. It is unclear whether there was an actual membership list or merely an informal nucleus augmented by constantly changing invitation lists. However, contemporary observers not privy to the meetings regarded the Breakfast Society as a significant link between the 'new bureaucrats' and the army faction led by General Nagata, and between these groups and such peers as Konoe, Kido, and Harada.

Despite their influential connections through the Kokuikai and the Breakfast Society, the 'new bureaucrats' were still a very small minority within the higher civil service and several years passed before they had much impact on national policy. During the period of the Saitō cabinet, their most publicized undertaking was Gotō's 1933 proposal for farm relief appropriations. He had the enthusiastic support of 'new bureaucrats' in the Agriculture Ministry, and the active collaboration of the army under General Araki, but the proposal was rejected by the cabinet after Finance Minister Takahashi Korekiyo[25] insisted that Japan could not afford the cost.

In January 1935, as home minister in the Okada cabinet, Gotō established an economics division in each of the forty-seven prefectural governments.[26] This did not create any new regulatory power, but did provide more civil service positions to which rising 'new bureaucrats' could be appointed and in which they could promote more vigorous use of existing economic powers. The Okada cabinet also created two new super-bureaus that quickly became strongholds of the 'new bureaucrats', who saw a unique opportunity for collective action and influence disproportionate to their meager numerical strength, previously fragmented among several ministries.

The new units, responsible directly to the cabinet, were the Manchurian Affairs Bureau (Tai-Man Jimukyoku) and a national-policy planning agency known initially as the Cabinet Investigation Bureau (Naikaku Chōsakyoku).[27] Unlike other cabinet bureaus, these were designed not to provide services to the ministries but to co-ordinate related activities of several ministries, thus breaching the jurisdictional barriers within the higher civil service. Moreover, permission was given for appointing active-duty army and navy officers to staff

23 鈴木貞一
24 池田成彬
25 高橋是清

26 Imperial Ordinance 4 of January 18, 1935.
27 対満事務局, 内閣調査局

positions within these 'civilian' bureaus, breaching the traditional barrier between the civil and military services.[28] By this time, in the spring of 1935, the chief military allies of the 'new bureaucrats' were officers of the army's Control (Tōsei) faction.[29] General Nagata played a key role in the creation of the Cabinet Investigation Bureau, and in overcoming opposition to the inclusion of military officers in it; the first such officer appointed was Lieutenant Colonel Suzuki Teiichi, long a close associate of the 'new bureaucrats'.

All this aroused the ire of young extremists in the army's Imperial Way (Kōdō) faction.[30] Their propaganda had always put the civil service high on the list of their enemies, and they no longer saw any reason to regard 'new bureaucrats' as exceptions to the rule. One ringleader of the February 1936 insurrection charged that the 'new bureaucrats' were counter-revolutionaries who had no interest in true reform but wanted only to exploit for their own advantage the growing political power of the army. In a striking historical analogy, this young terrorist likened the 'new bureaucrats' of the 1930s to the men who in the 1860s had advocated *kōbu gattai*, or coalition between the imperial court and the Tokugawa shogunate.[31] In other words, the proponents of *kōbu gattai* had sought civilian help to save a corrupt military regime and avert the Meiji Restoration, while the 'new bureaucrats' were seeking military help to save a corrupt civilian regime and avert the Shōwa restoration which army dissidents were demanding.

The assassination of General Nagata in August 1935 and the near-success of the February 1936 insurrection had an ambivalent effect on the 'new bureaucrats'. Gotō Fumio (who had been marked for

---

[28] Before this time, hardly any military officers had served in civilian bureaus, partly because the emperor Meiji had enjoined the army and navy to remain aloof from political activity and partly because appointment to a civilian bureau resulted in automatic retirement from active military duty status. For the Manchurian Affairs Bureau, the Okada cabinet adopted the legal fiction that military personnel were not 'appointed' to it but merely 'assigned' *(ho)* and could therefore remain on active military status. For the Cabinet Investigation Bureau, the cabinet went a step farther,

enacting a new ordinance that authorized formal appointment of active-duty military officers to civilian posts.

[29] 統制派

[30] 皇道派

[31] *Gendaishi shiryō* 現代史資料 (Tokyo: Misuzu Shobō, 1962-), v (*Kokkashugi undō II* 国家主義運動), 770–1. The provenance of this document, written shortly before the rebellion, is explained on pp. xlii-xlv, 774. Part of it, including the passage cited above, was published in the March 1936 issue of *Nippon hyōron*.

assassination) and other prominent members of the first group left the government. However, their departure was more than offset by the emergence of younger men in the planning agency and the economic ministries, who accepted and indeed gloried in appellations setting them apart from other bureaucrats. In fact, they even professed to be different from the *shin kanryō* of the Saitō and Okada cabinets and wanted a new name. As early as July 1936, some were calling themselves *shin-shin kanryō* or 'new-new bureaucrats', prompting one critic to anticipate at least half-seriously the emergence of *chō kanryō* and *chō-chō kanryō*[32]—'super bureaucrats' and 'super-super bureaucrats'.[33] Others preferred the equivocal term *seinen kanryō* or 'young bureaucrats', inviting comparison with the rebellious *seinen shōkō* or 'young officers' of the army and navy. By 1937, however, the most popular term was *kakushin kanryō*,[34] literally 'reform bureaucrats' or 'renovation bureaucrats'. This expression was neither new nor unambiguous, since the earlier *shin kanryō* had often been described as part of a *kakushin undō* or 'reform movement', while the phrase *kakushin gumbu* or 'reformist military men'[35] usually referred to the revolutionary extremists.

Western writers, then and since, have ignored or overlooked this proliferation of Japanese names, and have stayed with the original term, 'new bureaucrats', without making more than feeble efforts at definition. Some Japanese historians have accepted the notion that there was some kind of qualitative change either in 1936 after the insurrection or in 1937 after the resumption of war with China, and have therefore tried to enforce a distinction between *shin kanryō* and *kakushin kanryō*. The objections to this are, first, that if there is a substantive difference it seems to be ineffable, and second, that the two terms have been used interchangeably in Japan for more than thirty years.[36]

---

[32] 新新官僚, 超官僚, 超超官僚

[33] 'Seinen kanri, shain wa nani o kangaete iru ka zadankai 青年官吏社員は何を考えているか座談会', *Bungei shunjū* 文藝春秋, XIV. 7 (July 1936), 219–20; and Itō, *Chūō kōron* 中央公論, LI.9, 117.

[34] 革新官僚

[35] 革新運動, 革新軍部

[36] Interchangeable use of the two expressions is not confined to those who see no difference between them. In 1958,

in signed articles in *Nihon kindaishi jiten* 日本近代史辞典 (Tokyo: Tōyō Keizai Shimpōsha, 1958), pp. 79, 285, Asada Mitsuteru 浅田光輝 postulated a chronological distinction between *shin kanryō* 新官僚 (active in 1932–7) and *kakushin kanryō* 革新官僚 (1937–45), but two years later as co-author (with Koyama Hirotake 小山弘健) of *Nihon teikoku-shugi shi* 日本帝国主義史 (Tokyo: Aoki Shoten, 1960), III, 84, 96, he ignored his*

If the Japanese terms are hopelessly and irretrievably confused, their literal translations into English are even less acceptable. For example, the term 'new bureaucrats' has accumulated many vague and contradictory definitions, while the term 'reform bureaucrats' is inherently tendentious, ambiguous, and value-laden. Consequently, I have elsewhere[37] proposed adoption of a new generic term, 're-visionist bureaucrats', to include all those who between 1932 and 1945 were called by any of the Japanese names mentioned above.[38] One advantage of the new name is that it recognizes similarities between men active at various times within this fourteen-year period, without excluding the possibility that valid subtypes may yet be identified. Another advantage is that the name 'revisionist' is politically neutral, implying only a desire for non-revolutionary change in the political, social, or economic order, and making no judgement of the merit or political coloration of the changes.

However, the complex problems of definition and evaluation are not solved simply by cutting through the thicket of Japanese terminological confusion. Despite the difficulty of identifying discrete subtypes, it is certain that the revisionists were never a well-defined group with agreed objectives and policies. Though less inhibited by sectional loyalties and more willing to collaborate across ministry boundaries, they resembled other bureaucrats in being highly susceptible to factionalism, and sometimes even the most closely knit factions developed internal strains. For example, in September 1934,

*own distinction and applied both names to the men of 1932–6.

[37] In 'The Bureaucracy as a Political Force', a paper prepared for the Sixth Seminar of the Conference on Modern Japan, at Fajardo, Puerto Rico, January 2–7, 1968. A revised version will appear in James W. Morley, ed., *Dilemmas of Growth in Prewar Japan*, to be published shortly by the Princeton University Press.

[38] The peculiarities of the problem are often overlooked. A few of the men called by one or more of these names conferred the title upon themselves. Most, however, acquired the label involuntarily through the reasoning or caprice of some journalist or politician; some welcomed the label while others resented or ques-

tioned it (see, for example, Matsumoto Manabu's 松本学 complaint in Itō, *Chūō kōron*, LI.9, 118–19). Any label applied so freely and casually, sometimes as a compliment and sometimes as a pejorative, and defined so rarely and inadequately, can only become more and more ambiguous. Moreover, some writers have fallen into the fallacy of implying that since 'new bureaucrats' emerged from Group A, and since X, Y, and Z were members of Group A, therefore X, Y, and Z were 'new bureaucrats'. In truth, of course, no one organization was composed solely of revisionists, and none included all the revisionists (however defined). Consequently, there is no agreed list of 'new bureaucrats'.

Police Bureau chief Karasawa Toshiki decided that his long-time friend and patron, Home Minister Gotō, was being dilatory in making personnel changes. He took the peculiar step of asking an outsider, Saionji's aide Harada, to prod Gotō to act.[39]

Such personal and tactical disagreements within or between factions make it harder to judge whether or how much the revisionists disagreed on goals or strategy. When some of the younger revisionists tried in the summer of 1936 to dissociate themselves from the original group led by Gotō, they could not agree on even the vaguest definition of their self-proclaimed 'newness'. One asserted that the original *shin kanryō* were unable to solve Japan's problem because their 'liberalism' *(riberarizumu)* committed them to laissez-faire capitalism. Yet, he said, the existing 'proletarian' parties were out of date, so what the *shin-shin kanryō* wanted was 'a complete Japanese transformation of socialism' based on Japan's unique 'national polity' *(kokutai)*. The murkiness of these comments was more than matched by another participant in the same roundtable discussion, who demanded that Japan's foreign policy be 'reoriented on a foundation of Japanese ideals as manifested in the Three Sacred Treasures' that constituted the imperial regalia.[40]

It is only fair to concede that this fog of obscurantism was occasionally pierced by a few concrete proposals, such as cancellation of farm debts, restriction of imports, and imposition of other economic controls. Even so, the contention by these men that they were fundamentally different from the Gotō group is not convincing. Their repeated references to the February 1936 insurrection as the dividing line between 'new' and 'new-new bureaucrats' strongly suggest that self-protection was their real concern. They had good reason to fear that army dissidents, though unsuccessful in February, might soon renew their attack on bureaucrats who were associated with General Nagata and his military heirs, as the Gotō group had been.

Even the growing emphasis on economic planning and control appears to have been due less to a qualitative change in revisionist thought than to obvious changes in circumstances and opportunities for action. The short-lived cabinet of General Hayashi Senjūrō

---

[39] Harada, IV, 64–5. Harada did as requested.

[40] 'Seinen kanri, shain wa nani o kangaete iru ka zadankai', *Bungei shunjū*, XIV.7, 220–3, 227.

transformed the Cabinet Investigation Bureau into a somewhat larger Cabinet Planning Agency (Kikakuchō),[41] in May 1937, and five months later the first Konoe cabinet combined the agency with another bureau to form a Cabinet Planning Board (Kikakuin)[42] with considerably enlarged responsibilities. One result was a conspicuous increase in the number of revisionist bureaucrats and in their ability to influence national policy. Revisionists appeared not only in the Planning Board, which became their foremost stronghold, but also within the ministries, even in such unlikely places as the Communications Ministry, where one of the first major economic control laws was drafted—the Electric Power Control Act of March 1938.

The most famous of the later revisionists were the 'Manchurian clique' of career bureaucrats whose political fortunes had profited enormously from temporary service in occupied Manchuria and collaboration there with General Tōjō Hideki[43] while he was Kwantung Army military police chief and chief of staff. This group, including Hoshino Naoki, Matsuoka Yōsuke, Kishi Nobusuke, Shiina Etsuzaburō, Ōhashi Chūichi, and Minobe Yōji,[44] returned to Japan one by one between 1938 and 1940, and moved into key positions at cabinet, sub-cabinet, and staff levels. They were especially conspicuous under the second Konoe cabinet, with Tōjō serving as war minister, Matsuoka as foreign minister, Hoshino as president of the Planning Board, Kishi and Ōhashi as vice ministers of commerce and foreign affairs, Shiina as a Commerce Ministry bureau chief, and Minobe on the Planning Board staff.

The methods and proposals of the 'Manchurian clique' were certainly more aggressive than those of the earlier Gotō faction of revisionists. Their free-wheeling experience in Manchuria's highly centralized regime had made them much more dissatisfied with the Japanese domestic system of divided political authority and minimal state intervention in the economy. But it is equally true that circumstances had changed greatly since 1934 or even 1936, because of the war in China and the growing prospect of a Pacific or Russian war. That the later revisionists felt both a greater urgency for and a greater capacity for changing the political and economic system

41 林銑十郎, 企画庁
42 企画院
43 東条英機

44 星野直樹, 松岡洋右, 岸信介, 椎名悦三郎, 大橋忠一, 美濃部洋次

does not prove that they were necessarily very different from the earlier revisionists, though some of them probably were.

Early or late, the revisionists have nearly always been classified as a segment of the right wing. For example, a December 1938 diagram of 'left- and right-wing organizations' by Kōno Tsuneyoshi described the *shin kanryō* as 'having links with the right-wing reformist camp' *(kakushin jin'ei)* as distinguished from the right-wing nationalist or 'patriotic camp' *(aikoku jin'ei).*[45] This distinction is echoed—with the same misleading implication that the two terms are mutually exclusive—by several postwar Japanese writers, who contrast 'the ideological right-wing (Japanist faction)' and 'the organized or reformist right-wing (national socialist faction)'.[46]

Evaluation of the revisionist bureaucrats as right-wing reformers has been so generally accepted that any sharp disagreement has shock value if nothing else. The most sweeping dissent from the usual view came from Prince Konoe, who in an impassioned statement to the emperor in February 1945 asserted that 'the so-called *shin kanryō* . . . consciously harbor the intention of bringing about a Red revolution. . . . The so-called right wing consists of Communists wearing a national-polity disguise.'[47] Seven months earlier, Konoe had told other former prime ministers that he 'feared a left-wing revolution more than loss of the war, because the imperial house and

[45] 河野恒吉， 革新陣営， 愛国陣営. Kido Nikki Kenkyūkai 木戸日記研究会, comp., *Kido Kōichi kankei bunsho* 木戸幸一関係文書 (Tokyo: Tōkyō Daigaku Shuppankai, 1966), pp. 465–7. Kōno was a retired infantry general then serving as a contributing editor of *Asahi shimbun* 朝日新聞. He sent the diagram and other documents to House of Peers member Baron Itō Bunkichi 伊藤文吉, who passed them to Kido on December 8, 1938.

[46] See, for example, Kinoshita Hanji 木下半治, 'Uyoku dantai 右翼団体', in *Nihon rekishi daijiten* 日本歴史大辞典, rev. ed. (Tokyo: Kawade Shobō, 1968–), I, 615 (from which the quoted wording is translated); the same author's 'Uyoku undō 右翼運動', in *Nihon kindaishi jiten*, p. 40; Okada Takeo 岡田丈夫, *Konoe Fumimaro: tennō to gumbu to kokumin* 天皇と軍部と国民 (Tokyo: Shunjūsha,

1959), p. 227; and Ishida Takeshi 石田雄, *Kindai Nihon seiji kōzō no kenkyū* 近代日本政治構造の研究 (Tokyo: Miraisha, 1956), p. 260.

[47] The complete text of this February 14, 1945 memorial is recorded in *Kido Kōichi kankei bunsho*, pp. 495–7; Yabe Teiji 矢部貞治, *Konoe Fumimaro* (Tokyo: Kōbundō, 1952), II, 529–33; and Robert J. C. Butow, *Japan's Decision to Surrender* (Stanford: Stanford University Press, 1954), pp. 47–50, with some variations in wording; all three versions contain the words translated above. This was Konoe's first private meeting with the emperor since October 1941, and Kido was the only other person present. It was the third in a series of meetings in which the emperor, on his own initiative, conferred individually with former prime ministers on the deteriorating war situation.

the national polity could survive' the latter but not the former.[48]

This highly unfavorable view of the revisionists is startling not merely because it is novel but especially because it came from the man who, more than any other, helped the revisionists to become a powerful force within the government. Konoe had been close to the revisionists from the beginning. He was a member of both the Kokuikai and the 1931–5 Breakfast Society, from which the first revisionists emerged, and he had been a friend of their leader, Gotō Fumio, since 1917.[49] When his closest political aides formed two 'brain trust' organizations in his behalf—the Shōwa Research Society and the 1937–40 Breakfast Society—several prominent revisionist bureaucrats were included.[50] Leaders of these two groups also established a Shōwa Academy (Shōwa Juku)[51] where 're-education' lectures were given to young revisionists and university students.

A secret paper prepared by the Shōwa Research Society in December 1936 complained that the *shin kanryō* were much less powerful than the public supposed, but predicted that 'hereafter the *shin kanryō* will gradually become powerful, and together with the military services they will be influential in opening a new era.'[52] Six months later, Konoe became prime minister, and in October 1937 he gave the revisionists the power base they needed, by combining the

[48] Kido Kōichi, *Kido Kōichi nikki* 木戸 幸一日記 (Tokyo: Tōkyō Daigaku Shuppankai, 1966), ii, 1125. The statement was made on July 18, 1944 at a meeting with Kido, Privy Council President Hara, and former prime ministers Wakatsuki, Okada, Hirota, Hiranuma, Abe, and Yonai, convened to choose a replacement for Tōjō.

[49] Furuta Tokujirō 古田徳次郎, 'Konoe no burein torasuto: kō o meguru hitobito 近衛のブレーン・トラスト: 公を めぐる人々', *Chūō kōron*, lii.7 (July 1937), 280–1.

[50] The Shōwa Research Society (Shōwa Kenkyūkai 昭和研究会) was organized by Gotō Ryūnosuke 後藤 隆之助 as a national-policy research and planning group in support of Konoe. It is usually dated from November 1936, but a contemporary account by Furuta Tokujirō described it as having been formed in September 1933, later disbanded, and revived in the fall of 1936. The *Kido Kōichi kankei bunsho* includes five documents from 1934 and 1935 attributed to the SRS. The later Breakfast Society was formed in November 1937 by Konoe's two private secretaries, Ushiba Tomohiko 牛場友彦 and Kishi Michizō 岸道三, as a kind of inner circle of the SRS. It seems to have had no connection with the earlier Breakfast Society; the revisionists who participated in the two were not the same men. See Furuta, *Chūō kōron*, lii.7, 277–8; Kazama Michitarō 風間道太郎, *Ozaki Hotsumi den* 尾崎秀実伝 (Tokyo: Hōsei Daigaku Shuppankyoku, 1968), pp. 239–44, 273–5; and Chalmers A. Johnson, *An Instance of Treason: Ozaki Hotsumi and the Sorge Spy Ring* (Stanford: Stanford University Press, 1964), pp. 114–17, 125–7.

[51] 昭和塾

[52] *Kido Kōichi kankei bunsho*, p. 235.

Resources Bureau with the Planning Agency to form the more potent Cabinet Planning Board.

The first project of the new Board was the drafting of the National General Mobilization Law, by which the Diet agreed to a sweeping delegation of authority to impose economic controls on labor and capital by executive ordinance alone. This crucial legislation was denounced by Saionji and various Diet members as flagrantly unconstitutional, and only Konoe's personal intervention pushed it through the Diet.[53] His close association with revisionist bureaucrats was shown also by several high-level appointments during his first and second terms as prime minister, and especially by his bringing the 'Manchurian clique' into high office in Japan.

On the other hand, revisionists were always a minority within Konoe's motley entourage. His friends and associates, often chosen with singular lack of discretion, ranged from socialists and 'converted' Communists to extreme conservatives. Partly for this reason, Konoe sometimes seemed intent on riding off in all directions at once. Within the span of a few months in 1937–8, he was personally engaged in such disparate projects as clandestine collaboration with Asō Hisashi[54] of the Socialist Masses Party, spearheading the revisionist drive for the Mobilization Law, seeking imperial amnesty for the February 1936 insurrectionists, and trying to make ultranationalist Tōyama Mitsuru[55] a cabinet counselor with rank equal to that of a minister of state.[56]

Moreover, Konoe was always sympathetic toward army officers of the Imperial Way faction, which had moved from dislike of non-revisionist bureaucrats to dislike of all bureaucrats and especially of revisionists. The evolution of Konoe's attitude was similar, though much slower. In his first cabinet, while working hand in glove with revisionists, Konoe made frequent indiscriminately derogatory remarks about the civil service, antagonizing some of his own appointees and alarming Saionji, who sent him a sharp rebuke.[57] He ridiculed the 'bureaucratic' manner of such close friends as Kido and sought

---

[53] Harada, vi, 243–6, 249–51, 262, 269 and Yabe, I, 473–80.

[54] 麻生久

[55] 頭山満

[56] George O. Totten iii, *The Social Democratic Movement in Prewar Japan* (New Haven: Yale University Press, 1966), pp. 102–7; Harada, vi, 76–87, 91, 105–7, 113, 116, 122–3, 126–8, 214, 217–20, 223–4; and Kazami Akira 風見章, *Konoe naikaku* 近衛内閣 (Tokyo: Nihon Shuppan Kyōdō KK, 1951), pp. 244–7.

[57] Harada, vi, 222; vii, 31, 105, 203.

persistently to expand loopholes in the merit system so that more non-careerists could be brought into the government. His disenchantment with revisionists seems to have begun with the discovery that they were not as atypical as he had supposed. Like other career bureaucrats, they resented his tampering with the civil service appointment regulations.[58]

The transformation of Konoe's attitude toward revisionists was undoubtedly accelerated by the trauma of two major scandals in his last year as prime minister: the Planning Board 'incident' and the Sorge spy case. In the former, seventeen officials of the Cabinet Planning Board were arrested on March 28, 1941 for Communist activity. In the latter, an important member of Konoe's entourage, Ozaki Hotsumi, was arrested on October 15, 1941 as a Soviet spy.[59] Konoe resigned as prime minister one day later, though largely for other reasons.

Most of the revisionists arrested in the Planning Board case were comparatively low-ranking non-careerists who had been brought into the civil service as 'researchers' *(chōsakan)* after the first Konoe cabinet relaxed the appointment regulations.[60] They came under fire as drafters of the second Konoe cabinet's plan for a 'new economic structure' under tight official control. Three of them—Wada Hiroo, Katsumata Seiichi, and Sata Tadataka[61]—became prominent after the war as left-wing Socialist members of the Diet. However, the chief sponsors of the 1941 plan were two of the Manchurian revisionists, Planning Board President Hoshino Naoki[62] and Commerce Vice Minister Kishi Nobusuke, who were not charged in the case.

In the Sorge spy ring, the information collected by Ozaki came partly from the files of Konoe's private secretaries and his first chief cabinet secretary, Kazami Akira,[63] to which Ozaki enjoyed free

---

58 Kazami, pp. 153. 240–2.

59 尾崎秀実. Yabe, II, 189–91, 195, 197–212; Okada, pp. 239–40; Kazama, pp. 325–6. Totten states (p. 245n) that 'when the Sorge spy ring was discovered in 1941, the police became extremely suspicious and arrested a number of members of the Planning Board (this is known as the Planning Board incident).' However, Japanese sources indicate a reverse sequence for these two events.

60 調査官. The chief exception was

Wada Hiroo 和田博雄, a career bureaucrat who had achieved section-chief rank in the Agriculture Ministry before transferring to the Planning Board. For a list of the seventeen arrested, see Shisō no Kagaku Kenkyūkai 思想の科学研究会, *Tenkō* 転向 (Tokyo: Heibonsha, 1959–60), II, 74.

61 勝間田清一, 佐多忠隆

62 星野直樹

63 風見章

E

access, and partly from the Shōwa Research Society and the Breakfast Society, in both of which Ozaki was very active. Well before its dissolution in 1940, the SRS had come under frequent attack as Communist-oriented, and most of the revisionist bureaucrats connected with it had prudently withdrawn.[64] However, at least six of the men arrested in the Planning Board case had been SRS members to the end. When Ozaki was exposed as both a Communist and a spy, Konoe's own reputation was gravely jeopardized.[65] In reaction, having learned too late the folly of trusting Ozaki, Konoe became suspicious of almost everyone who had any connection with the SRS. And though no bureaucrats were implicated in the Sorge case,[66] his mistrust soon extended to revisionist bureaucrats in general.

The intensity of his suspicions can be gauged from a number of conversations involving former prime minister Okada's son-in-law, Sakomizu Hisatsune,[67] who was a prominent revisionist of high rank, close to Kishi Nobusuke and others of the Manchurian group. By the spring of 1944, for reasons still somewhat obscure, both Sakomizu and Kishi had turned against Tōjō. Knowing that Konoe was anxious to oust the Tōjō cabinet, Sakomizu remarked to him that since there seemed to be no easy way of getting rid of Tōjō, the only alternative was to try to govern as badly as possible. Konoe considered this idea 'very suspicious', even if meant as a jest.[68]

[64] Kazama, p. 240. Ozaki was also a regular lecturer in the Shōwa Academy.

[65] Although there is no reason to believe that Konoe knew of Ozaki's duplicity, he could not escape the obloquy of having made it easy for 'Communism to penetrate even the cabinet itself', in the harsh phrase of Count Makino Nobuaki 牧野伸顕. Konoe was interrogated at length about his connections with Ozaki and others involved in the spy ring, and he gave answers that were less than the whole truth. Except for his close ties with the imperial family, he would probably have been arrested (as some senior military officers demanded and as he himself feared). See *Tenkō*, II, 105; Kazami, pp. 259–61; Johnson, pp. 179–80; and F. W. Deakin and G. R. Storry, *The Case of Richard Sorge* (New York:

Harper & Row, 1966), pp. 190–2, 278–9, 294.

[66] Ozaki (sentenced to death), Saionji Kinkazu 西園寺公一 (two-year sentence, suspended), and Inukai Ken 犬養健 (acquitted) had all been employed as 'consultants' (*shokutaku* 嘱託) by the government, but none can be considered a bureaucrat in the normal sense.

[67] 迫水久常

[68] Hosokawa Morisada 細川護貞, *Jōhō tennō ni tassezu* 情報天皇に達せず (Tokyo: Dōkōsha Isobe Shobō, 1953), I, 174, 189. Sakomizu seems to have had a penchant for ambiguity, as further illustrated by a 1945 incident described by Butow, pp. 167–8, 204–5, and a statement attributed to him by Maruyama Masao 丸山真男, *Thought and Behaviour in Modern Japanese Politics* (London: Oxford University Press,*

The nature of Konoe's suspicion was made clear by the context in which he mentioned this conversation to his son-in-law, Hosokawa Morisada.[69] When Hosokawa told him of a naval officer's assertion that Sakomizu was 'Red', Konoe said he had heard similar disquieting comments from two Imperial Way generals, Yanagawa Heisuke and Obata Toshishirō,[70] and that he himself had recently had this curious conversation with Sakomizu. A month later (June 7, 1944), he told Hosokawa about a conversation with Kido, who had been a staunch supporter of Tōjō but was becoming worried about 'penetration of the Railway and Finance Ministries by Reds', and wondered 'whether Sakomizu may not be one of these'.[71] A year later, Sakomizu became chief cabinet secretary in the Suzuki cabinet, on the recommendation of Admiral Okada but over the objections of former prime ministers Yonai and Hiranuma. Criticizing this appointment and that of Akinaga Tsukizō as chief of the cabinet's Composite Planning Bureau, Konoe complained that 'once again the *kakushin kanryō* will run rampant,' and because of this, 'the new cabinet's prospects are dark.'[72]

Konoe's hostile evaluation of the revisionists in 1944–5 is easily disparaged as the overreaction of a man who felt frustrated and betrayed. He was wrong about Sakomizu,[73] and his blanket indictment of revisionists as Communist revolutionaries is insupportable. However, postwar Japanese writers are no more perceptive when they dismiss the revisionists as just another group of fascists. Aside from their ambiguity, both labels ignore the heterogeneity of revisionists and the similarities between fascism and Communism.

Most revisionists shared some important characteristics. For

---

*1963), p. 123: 'A public servant must be a deliberate opportunist. Even if he should seem to have a certain ideology, this must be related, not to his personality, but to his "position".'

69 細川護貞,

70 柳川平助, 小畑敏四郎

71 Hosokawa, I, 214–15.

72 *Suzuki Kantarō den* 鈴木貫太郎伝 (Tokyo: Suzuki Kantarō Denki Hensan Iinkai 鈴木貫太郎伝記編纂委員会, 1960), pp. 186–7; and Okada Keisuke 岡田啓介, *Kaikoroku* 回顧録 (Tokyo: Mainichi Shimbunsha, 1950), p. 236. Akinaga 秋永月三, who had been a section chief in the Planning Board while Konoe was prime minister, was not a civilian but a general; however, Konoe said in his February 1945 memorial that he considered military men to be 'putty in the hands' of the *shin kanryō*.

73 Sakomizu's views in 1945 on ending the war seem similar to Konoe's; see Butow, *passim*, and F. C. Jones, *Japan's New Order in East Asia* (London: Oxford University Press, 1954), p. 423. Since the war, Sakomizu has won election five times to the Diet as a member of the conservative party, and he served in the first and second Ikeda cabinets.

example, they were university graduates of superior ability, they had won admission to the inner elite of the career bureaucracy by passing formidable examinations, and they wanted to make changes. But they varied considerably in political orientation and therefore in the kind of changes sought, the methods preferred, and the allies accepted. Chalmers Johnson said of the largely non-bureaucratic Shōwa Research Society that it 'included liberals, ultranationalists, Communists, Marxists, opportunists, and several men committed only to bureaucratic roles'.[74] This description applies also to the revisionist bureaucrats, except that the proportion of Communists and Marxists seems to have been much smaller, and of course the six types mentioned were not mutually exclusive.

The usual similarities between the radical left and right were intensified in Japan by two countervailing forces: a highly eclectic receptivity to diverse European political and economic ideas and an obsession with appearing always to be distinctively Japanese. Substance and style were easily confused. For example, one young man boasted in 1936 (under cloak of anonymity) that he and his friends were 'new-new bureaucrats . . . the vanguard of Japanese fascism', but attributed their social awareness to Communist indoctrination on university campuses in the 1920s, because of which he was 'extremely grateful to Communism'.[75] This was the same man who thought that Japan's foreign policy ought to be based on the Three Sacred Treasures of Shinto mythology and dedicated to 'the eradication of Communism from the world'. Who can say whether such a man was a convert from Communism (*tenkōsha*), a sham convert (*gisō tenkōsha*),[76] or merely a fuzzy thinker with romantic delusions?

Revisionist statements about their goals are either too nebulous or too equivocal to be of probative value. Of course, this is true also of the young officers and the civilian radicals, but unlike those groups, the revisionists were constantly and directly involved in national policy, planning, and administration. Their purposes and tactics are therefore susceptible to much more objective investigation than might be indicated by the simplistic labels and impressionistic ver-

---

74 Johnson, p. 116. Similarly, Deakin and Storry (p. 192) say of the SRS that 'some members . . . were nationalists; others were socialists, non-Marxist and Marxist'. This description too would fit the revisionists as a group.

75 'Seinen kanri, shain wa nani o kangaete iru ka zadankai', *Bungei shunjū*, XIV.7, 226, 234–5.

76 転向者, 擬装転向者

dicts of Japanese writers. Case studies of major laws and ordinances of 1932–45, identifying their chief architects and sponsors, and indicating what compromises were made, would do much to clarify the political mixture within the revisionist camp and the extent to which subtypes within the group are definable. Although research in legislative history is far more difficult for Japan than for any country with either a strong parliament or a truly centralized executive authority, the task is gradually being made more feasible by the publication of relevant documents.[77]

The present insufficiency of evidence about the strategy and objectives of the revisionists does not, however, prevent recognition of their historical importance. A prime clue to this was suggested long ago, in a comment on their first major undertaking—the unsuccessful 1933 proposal for farm relief. A shrewd observer remarked that when Gotō Fumio 'and General Araki and their respective disciples met . . . it was the bureaucrats who held the upper hand, because they had precise plans and the army did not.'[78] A similar insight was implicit in Saionji's warning to Konoe in 1938 that the business of government was manageable only by career bureaucrats, 'and not by the army or political parties'.[79] By 1945, Konoe himself had come to believe that 'our ignorant and simple-minded military men are putty in the hands' of revisionist bureaucrats.[80] Though this was hyperbole, it had a core of realism.

The constitutional system contrived by the Meiji oligarchs insured the fragmentation of political power among several elites, none able to govern alone. The military services had one major advantage: legally exempt from civilian control, they could change foreign policy by unilateral action outside Japan. Short of destroying the Meiji system itself, they could not change domestic policy without the help of some other elite group. After February 1936,

---

[77] See, for example, Ishikawa Junkichi 石川準吉, comp., *Sōgō kokusaku to kyōiku kaikakuan: Naikaku Shingikai, Naikaku Chōsakyoku kiroku* 総合国策と教育改革案: 内閣審議会, 内閣調査局記録 (Tokyo: Shimizu Shoin, 1962); and the Defense Agency War History Office's projected ninety-volume history of World War II, *Senshi sōsho* 戦史叢書 (Tokyo: Asagumo Shimbunsha, 1966–), especially such volumes as *Rikugun gunju dōin: keikaku hen* 陸軍軍需動員: 計画編 (1967), pp. 548–638, and the forthcoming *Rikugun gunju dōin: jisshi hen*. 陸軍軍需動員: 実施編

[78] Minoru Uchida, 'Japan as a Totalitarian State', *Amerasia* II.3 (May 1938), 135.

[79] Harada, VI, 222.

[80] Memorial of February 14, 1945; see footnote 47 above.

when the army decided against revolution, the coalition between the military and the revisionist bureaucrats was stronger than any alternative combination of elites, because each supplied what the other lacked.

In short, the army-revisionist partnership was not as unequal as outward signs suggested. Despite their mastery of propaganda and coercion, few military officers had the knowledge and procedural skills required for effective non-military planning and administration. Behind its arrogance and bombast, the army was compelled to rely on revisionist bureaucrats for much of its domestic program. Conversely, with army backing the revisionists could enact legislation they could never have pushed through alone. Each half of the coalition remained doubtful of the other's motives and uncertain whether it was manipulating or being manipulated. Still, the alliance rested on a real or imagined concurrence of objectives, as well as a recognition of the practical benefits of collaboration. Its ultimate collapse resulted not from internal tension but from external catastrophe.

Restoration
History and Shōwa Politics

GEORGE M. WILSON

IT is commonplace to acknowledge that history never repeats itself: no matter how tempting the parallels between one set of historical events and another may become, at some point still relatively high on the scale of generalization the differences begin to outweigh the similarities, and one process is seen to be distinct from the other. But if it is true that history does not repeat itself, then it is equally true that historical actors often think it does. They frequently decide that historical analogy is the most convenient method for explaining to themselves and others what an unfolding set of events 'really' means.

Of all the historical precedents that have appealed to Japanese during the past hundred years, none comes close in popularity to the Meiji Restoration and the events leading up to it. The typical pattern is that men who have looked back to the Restoration have wanted to repeat it, to rectify present wrongs by doing the Restoration over again. They have hoped, in short, to accomplish what they understood as the 'real' purpose of the Restoration.

After the death of Emperor Meiji in 1912, young men discontent with the inequalities of an urbanizing and industrializing Japan often raised the call for a 'Taishō restoration'. Asahi Heigo, for example, the fanatic who in 1921 murdered financial tycoon Yasuda Zenjirō, was found with a letter in his pocket explaining his action: 'My fellow young idealists! Your mission is to bring about a Taishō Restoration.' The means to this end were to be those of the resolute patriots of *bakumatsu* years (1853–68): 'Simply stab, stick, cut, and shoot. There is no need to meet or organize. Just sacrifice your life.'[1] The objects of the called-for campaign of terror were not foreigners or hated Bakufu leaders, as in *bakumatsu* times, but capitalists and 'venal' party politicians.

---

[1] 朝日平吾, 安田善次郎. *Sources of Japanese Tradition* (New York: Columbia University Press, 1964), II, 261–2.

The 1930s brought a veritable flood of demands for a 'Shōwa restoration', as Mr. Shillony, in particular, has shown in his article on the young officers of the February 26 (1936) Affair. But this era also produced so much disorder that people were reminded of the years leading up to the Restoration, giving rise to a host of analogies between the political history of the Restoration and the political crises of the 1930s. Mr. Spaulding notes in his article on the 'revisionist bureaucrats' that one of the rebel officers in 1936 drew 'a striking historical analogy' between the new-bureaucrat types and those Bakufu officials who subscribed to the idea of 'union between Court and Bakufu' *(kōbu gattai)*.[2] There was nothing rare about this kind of analogy. Men of various persuasions pointed out apparent similarities between *bakumatsu* events and those of the mid-1930s. Statesmen and party leaders vied with military officers in making direct comparisons and predicting analogous outcomes for present problems. Even foreign observers sometimes jumped on the bandwagon.[3]

We will do well to examine this phenomenon, for the men who posited such analogies were serious in purpose: they saw their world at least in significant part as a repetition of what they thought to have happened three quarters of a century earlier on the eve of the Meiji Restoration. However much historians might wish to criticize their historical biases, we can all learn from them something of the self-image of their own time.

The grossest imputation of identity between Restoration history and Shōwa politics that I have encountered occurs in a document appended to Hata Ikuhiko's book, *A History of the Military Fascist Movement*. This particular document has the title 'The Ansei purge of Shōwa', and it bears the date June 1935.[4] It was written by a person or persons who were obviously sympathetic to the generals of the

---

2 公武合体

3 For example, Hugh Byas, *Government by Assassination* (New York: Alfred A. Knopf, 1942), pp. 119–20, argues that the emperor feared the February 26 rebellion as a harbinger of the coming of a new Bakufu, in other words, as the undoing of the Meiji Restoration: 'Hirohito knew the history of his own house, and the skeleton in the Imperial cupboard was the dread of a new shogunate in khaki uniforms. How

can any Japanese emperor forget the humiliations his ancestors suffered from military chieftains. . .?'

4 'Shōwa no Ansei taigoku' 昭和の安政大獄, Appendix No. 11, in Hata Ikuhiko 秦郁彦, *Gun fuashizumu undō shi* 軍ファシズム運動史 (Tokyo: Kawade Shobō Shinsha, 1962), pp. 274–5. All translations from this document come from the above place and therefore will receive no further acknowledgement in footnotes.

Kōdō (Imperial Way) faction of the army, and although its exact provenance is not disclosed it could even be the product of Isobe Asaichi or Muranaka Kōji,[5] the two young officers who were discharged from service in the aftermath of the Military Academy Incident of November 1934 and who later came to play key roles in the February 26 Affair.

Before looking at this remarkable document, it may be useful to summarize the events, verified and unverified, that attended the Military Academy Incident.[6] Late in 1934, Captains Isobe and Muranaka (the latter of whom had been enrolled in the War College, a highly prestigious assignment for a young officer) conceived a grandiose plan to smash the existing government and replace it by direct military rule. In execution, the plan followed the lines of the ultimately unsuccessful May 15 (1932) Affair. The plotters planned to coordinate murders of high public officials with the takeover of key points throughout downtown Tokyo in such a way that the military would have to assume national control in order to guarantee stability. This plan depended on the cooperation of a number of other young officers and also cadets at the Military Academy. Unlike the makers of the May 15 Affair, however, Isobe and Muranaka did not keep silence about their plan until they could launch it, but instead discussed its details with two officers outside of their regular circle, Captain Tsuji Masanobu,[7] an instructor at the Military Academy, and Major Katakura Chū,[8] assigned to the Military Affairs Bureau of the War Ministry, which was controlled by Major General Nagata Tetsuzan.[9] Although Tsuji and Katakura spent much effort trying to dissuade the plotters from undertaking their scheme, Isobe and Muranaka remained adamant, and eventually their plans were reported to higher authorities. For undisclosed reasons a court martial decided against delivering an indictment and instead ordered that Isobe and Muranaka be quietly dismissed from the army. The public was left in the dark, and the facts of this incident did not become generally known until after the Pacific War.

5 磯部浅一, 村中孝次

6 On the Military Academy Incident, see Hata, pp. 99–106; Takahashi Masae 高橋正衛, *Ni ni-roku jiken: 'Shōwa ishin' no shisō to kōdō* 二・二六事件——昭和維新' の思想と行動 (Tokyo: Chūō Kōronsha, 1965), pp. 129–31; and James B. Crowley, *Japan's Quest for Autonomy: National Security and Foreign Policy, 1930–1938* (Princeton: Princeton University Press, 1966), pp. 257–8.

7 辻政信

8 片倉衷

9 永田鉄山

Beyond this bare factual outline, the truth of the matter is hidden by misinformation, innuendo, and surmise. The plotters accused higher officers of using the plot for political ends.[10] And the document called 'The Ansei purge of Shōwa' illustrates the conspirators' conviction that Major General Nagata, head of the Military Affairs Bureau and 'brain' of the Tōsei (Control) faction, had distorted the incident at the Military Academy into a device for destroying the prestige of Generals Araki Sadao and Mazaki Jinzaburō, heroes of the Imperial Way faction.

'The Ansei purge of Shōwa' opens with a reminder to the reader that the original Ansei purge lasted from mid-1858 to the end of 1859 and that, 'for the loyalist patriot, it was a time of gnashing teeth and painful indignation.' (Indeed it was: this was the time when the *tairō* or great councillor of the Bakufu, Ii Naosuke of Hikone, tired of the machinations of rivals for power such as Tokugawa Nariaki of Mito and Matsudaira Shungaku of Fukui, placed them under house arrest and then hunted down their followers all over Japan, often executing them; such latterday heroes as Yoshida Shōin of Chōshū, the scholar and terrorist, were among the *tairō*'s victims; and more seasoned and rational reformers like Hashimoto Sanai of Fukui also died on Ii's orders.)[11] At present, the text continues, a terrible new purge 'worse than the Ansei purge' has begun within the army, which the author or authors vilify by calling it 'essentially the center' of a new Bakufu.

Heroes and villains presently take the stage as we read further in 'The Ansei purge of Shōwa'. Chief among the villains, of course, is Major General Nagata, who is cast in the part of Manabe Akikatsu, the *fudai* lord of Sabae whom Ii Naosuke appointed senior councillor in mid-1858 and sent to Kyoto with orders to root out and punish 'extremists' in the imperial capital.[12] Nagata's henchmen turn out to be modern reincarnations of other *bakumatsu* antiheroes: Major Katakura Chū is Nagano Shuzen,[13] Ii Naosuke's confidant and a man whom Murdoch likened to Fouché, although 'morally perhaps he is a better man than Fouché',[14] while Captain Tsuji Masanobu is

10 Hata, pp. 104–5.

11 大老，井伊直弼，彦根，徳川斉昭，水戸，松平春嶽，福井，吉田松陰，長州，橋本左内

12 間部詮勝，譜代，鯖江

13 長野主膳

14 James Murdoch, *A History of Japan*, III (London: Kegan Paul, Trench, Trubner, 1926), 678. Fouché was the linchpin of the effort to destroy Robes-*

the Bakufu spy in Kyoto, a colorful figure called Bunkichi.[15] The object of this twentieth-century Bakufu cabal is to eliminate true loyalism in the army: 'The modern Akikatsu [Nagata] clad in a khaki-colored uniform secretly plans to suppress the young officers with the help of Ii's confidant, Nagano Shuzen [Katakura]. Shuzen is contriving all sorts of crafty intrigues for detecting agitation among young officers throughout the country.'

Next, the heroes enter onto the stage. General Araki Sadao, former war minister and doyen of the Imperial Way faction, takes the part of the grand old lord of Mito, Tokugawa Nariaki himself, in all his *sonnō jōi* splendor.[16] 'In order to ensnare loyal generals . . . , [Nagata and company] have circulated rumors saying that "the Araki group of generals plots intrigues by using the young officers," and they have publicized this as "the treachery *(gomuhon)* of Mito *rōkō*[17] [Tokugawa Nariaki]".'

Instead of pursuing *bakumatsu* loyalists in Kyoto, this time Nagano Shuzen and the undercover man Bunkichi (Katakura and Tsuji) go forth and arrest Isobe and Muranaka at the Military Academy in Ichigaya, in downtown Tokyo, early in the morning of November 20, 1934. (In fact, the military police made the arrests.) This incident is labeled as the first of several Ansei purges of the Shōwa period.[18] (General Mazaki had accused Nagata of planting Tsuji in the Military Academy as an agent provocateur. Tsuji's task was presumably to create a pretext for smearing Mazaki and causing him to have to resign his post as inspector general of military education.)

Still another purge had occurred early in 1935, according to 'The Ansei purge of Shōwa', when Akikatsu (Nagata) conspired with 'a court noble' named Gotō (Gotō Fumio, the home minister) to suppress those who were patriotically condemning Minobe Tatsukichi's emperor-organ theory. Gotō thus unwillingly assumes the role of Kujō Hisatada, the pro-Bakufu first minister *(kampaku)* of the imperial court at the time of the Ansei purge, who was the *bête noire* of all the loyalists.[19] (Gotō is parenthetically labeled a 'new

*pierre. Brinton writes that 'Fouché was a man of great intelligence and no morals'; Crane Brinton, *A Decade of Revolution, 1789–1799* (New York: Harper & Row, 1934), p. 191.

15 文吉

16 尊皇攘夷

17 御謀叛，水戸老公

18 市ケ谷，安政，昭和

19 後藤文夫，関白，美濃部達吉，九条尚忠

bureaucrat,' reminding us of Mr. Spaulding's comment that the rebel officers lost no love for such types.)

The document concludes with dire predictions of yet a third round of purges to come. Nagata, it says, will report to his chief, Ii Naosuke, perhaps as early as August 1935 when the War Ministry would announce the annual roster of periodic transfers. Who is Ii Naosuke? He turns out to be a combination of Generals Ugaki Kazushige and Minami Jirō,[20] two former war ministers who were very unpopular with the young officers because of their earlier actions that discouraged the prospects for direct military rule. Ugaki and Minami were then on duty, respectively, in Korea and Manchuria. This double Ii would authorize Nagata to crack down anew on the young officers who favored 'sonnō tōbaku' (revere the emperor, overthrow the Bakufu),[21] and the result would be the complete takeover of power in the army by the 'sabaku' (pro-Bakufu) group,[22] that is, the Control faction.

For the young officers, the lesson should be clear. 'The patriotic and sincere warrior (*shi*) must resist no matter how severe the suppression and must dash forward bravely along the highway to the [Shōwa] restoration. We proclaim to patriotic warriors all over the realm (*tenka*) that the enemy of the restoration today is neither the *zaibatsu* nor the political parties, but a single gang of military staff officers who are the disciples and progeny of the *gumbatsu* [generals whom the young officers disliked].'

'The Ansei purge of Shōwa' ends before certain other parallels receive explicit attention. For example, if Nagata Tetsuzan was Manabe Akikatsu, and if Yoshida Shōin planned to kill Manabe, which he did, then Lieutenant Colonel Aizawa Saburō[23] must be the Yoshida Shōin of the 1930s (and then some), since he actually did succeed in killing Nagata in August 1935, before that predicted third purge could materialize.

But there is no need to continue along such epigrammatic lines. The point is that the officer or officers who seem to have written 'The Ansei purge of Shōwa' found conditions in the mid-1930s explicable only in terms of what happened during the *bakumatsu* period. The Bakufu is reborn as the Control faction, and loyalist emotions are invoked to justify terror against it.

20 宇垣一成, 南次郎
21 尊皇討幕

22 佐幕
23 士, 天下, 財閥, 軍閥, 相沢三郎

But this kind of explanation by historical analogy was not limited to military men. A party leader, for instance, Asō Hisashi of the Socialist Masses Party (Shakai Taishūtō),[24] viewed the fierce political struggles of the 1930s as directly analogous to *bakumatsu* factional strife.[25] He held that reformers in the various *han* generally came from among lower samurai, and that there was little unity between upper and lower samurai but only among lower samurai across a number of *han*. This led Asō to conclude that low-ranking military officers and younger government officials ('revisionist bureaucrats'?) were the 'lower samurai' of the 1930s. If they would act for the army and the civil bureaucracy (which to Asō made up the *tozama* daimyo group),[26] they could overcome the 'established parties' (*kisei seitō*),[27] which comprised the modern analogue of the Tokugawa administration.

Asō pushed the analogies between Restoration history and the 1930s rather far, and his viewpoint differed from that of the more violent agitators. Unlike Asahi Heigo and the rebels of February 1936, Asō saw no use in terrorism, which he condemned in the Restoration and also in the 1930s as mere 'individual action', ineffective for bringing about the desired reforms. However, as in so much of the historical thinking of men in the 1930s, the interesting thing about Asō's comparisons is not their specific content, but the fact that Restoration history had become the key for explaining current events.

What does all this tell us about the self-image of an era? First, quite obviously, it confirms that a crisis atmosphere prevailed in Japanese political circles, similar to that which men of the 1930s believed had existed in the decade prior to the Meiji Restoration. Second, it indicates that the crises of the 1930s, like those of the *bakumatsu* period, derived their fundamental character from internal power struggles rather than from foreign-policy problems, however significant was the catalytic role of the latter. The heroes and villains of the 1930s were Japanese pitted one against another, sometimes over issues of foreign policy but more often—as during the *bakumatsu* years—over domestic questions.

24 麻生久, 社会大衆党

25 My comments on Asō come by way of an article by William D. Wray called 'Asō Hisashi and the Search for Renovation in the 1930's', to be published in 1970 in *Papers on Japan* (Harvard University, East Asian Research Center, 1961–), v.

26 藩, 外様

27 既成政党

If there is a third lesson, whether relating to party leaders, new bureaucrats, old bureaucrats, young officers, or reservists both moderate and radical, it is perhaps this: the Restoration experience as interpreted by men of the 1930s had brought a sea change in Japanese political life; after years of disorder, the old regime gave way to one radically different in character. To put it another way, it seemed to suggest that a high level of domestic fragmentation, contradictory demands, and international tension could overload the capabilities of the political system and threaten its survival.[28] Men who view their present circumstances as a probable repetition of a radical change in the past may either like or dislike the prospects ahead; most men, especially political and military leaders, are apt to dislike them intensely and to fear impending catastrophe. It is likely that a thorough study of the kind of analogies I have been discussing would reveal that most members of the power elite were terribly apprehensive about the parallels they perceived between Restoration history and Shōwa politics.

To the extent that this is an accurate reading, it may help to explain the concern for law and order and stability that civilian and military authorities voiced in common so frequently after 1935. The conservative reaffirmation of the late 1930s was not a result of foreign difficulties but of internal strife. The losers were the radical young officers and the effusively patriotic local reservists. The winners were the Control-faction types in the military and also the civil bureaucracy. The crises of the mid-1930s gave them an opportunity to suppress social and political agitation and to go about achieving the process of gearing up the economy for maximum productivity and self-sufficiency—a process they hoped would bring the 'China incident' to an end and guarantee Japan's autonomy. That it did not is perhaps a measure of their failings, but that is another important question beyond the scope of this essay.

[28] In the sense discussed by Gabriel A. Almond and G. Bingham Powell, *Comparative Politics: A Developmental* *Approach* (Boston: Little, Brown, 1966), p. 194.

Index